ACTING SKILLS
FOR LAWYERS

Laura Mathis

ACTING SKILLS

FOR LAWYERS

LAURA MATHIS

Cover design by Daniel Mazanec/ABA Publishing

The materials contained herein represent the opinions and views of the authors and/or the editors, and should not be construed to be the views or opinions of the law firms or companies with whom such persons are in partnership with, associated with, or employed by the American Bar Association unless adopted pursuant to the bylaws of the Association.

Nothing contained in this book is to be considered as the rendering of legal advice for specific cases, and readers are responsible for obtaining such advice from their own legal counsel. This book and any forms and agreements herein are intended for educational and informational purposes only.

© 2011 American Bar Association. All rights reserved. No part of this publication may be reproduced, stored in a retrieval system, or transmitted in any form or by any means, electronic, mechanical, photocopying, recording, or otherwise, without the prior written permission of the publisher. For permission contact the ABA Copyrights & Contracts Department, copyright@abanet.org or via fax at (312) 988-6030.

15 14 13 12 11   5 4 3 2 1

Library of Congress Cataloging-in-Publication Data
Acting skills for lawyers / by Laura Mathis.
   p. cm.
   1. Trial practice—United States. 2. Acting. I. Title.
KF8915.M374 2011
347.73'504—dc23   2011024948
ISBN: 978-1-61632-932-7

Discounts are available for books ordered in bulk. Special consideration is given to state bars, CLE programs, and other bar-related organizations. Inquire at Book Publishing, ABA Publishing, American Bar Association, 321 North Clark Street, Chicago, Illinois 60654.

www.ababooks.org

Contents

Contents v

Introduction ix

Acknowledgments xiii

Chapter 1
The Art of Presence 1
Opening Statement: No One Will Listen If They Don't Know
    You're There 1
Stage Presents 1
Self-Sabotage 3
Developing Your Stage Presence 3
It Isn't Natural 4
Psychological Preparation 6
Utilize a Sense of Calm to Develop Stage Presence 7
Visualization 8
Athletes Do It Too 8
Can Stage Presence Really Be Learned? 9
My Killer Cat 10
The Quickie Way to Obtain Stage Presence 11
Avoid Betraying Your True Self 11
Do Your Research/Be Sneaky 13
Breaking Out of Your Shell 15
Closing Argument 17

Chapter 2
Vocal Variety and the Benefit of Keeping the Jury Awake 19
Opening Statement: You Can't Win If They Don't Listen 19
How Loud Should I Be? 21
Breathing 22
Relaxation 24
Articulation 25

v

Developing Articulation 26
Tongue Twisters 26
Vocal Variety 27
The Care of a Lawyer's Voice 31
Closing Argument 32

Chapter 3
Determine Your Character by Knowing Your Audience 33
Opening Statement: Know Yourself in Order to Be Yourself 33
Feeling Like an Ass 34
You Have to Say It Out Loud 35
Embrace What You Are! 35
Knowing Your Audience 36
The Courtroom 36
The Audience Has Left the Building 38
Determining Your Character 39
Applying Your Voice to the Chosen Attitude 42
Creating Relationships 43
Closing Argument 44

Chapter 4
Being in Your Body 45
Opening Statement: Effective Speech Delivery Involves
   the Whole Person 45
The Neutral Position 46
How Do You Know You Are In a Solid Neutral Position? 46
Remember: An Action Is Stronger Than a Word 48
"Do You Think I'm Sexy?" 48
Body Language: What Is the Story You Are Telling? 49
How to Act Like a Tough Guy 51
Gestures, or "Why Are My Arms So Long?" 53
Eye Contact 54
Closing Argument 55

Chapter 5
Taking Depositions/Being a Talk Show Host 57
Opening Statement: You're Exactly Like Larry King 57
Depositions in General 58
What You Don't Know CAN Hurt You 59
Hey, Come Here Often? 60
Don't Interrupt! 61

Keep It Open 62
When You Have More Time! 64
Dictate the Tempo of the Deposition 64
Call It Like You See It 65
Closing Argument 66

Chapter 6
Improvisation **67**
Opening Statement: Think Fast or Come In Last 67
Improvisation Skills 68
Warming Up 69
How to Improvise When Put on the Spot 71
How to Be Loose and Ready to Go 71
Your Body Will Improvise, Whether You Want It To or Not! ... 72
Explore and Heighten 74
Eye Contact and Grounding 77
Diction 77
How to Be Better at Improvisation 78
Closing Argument 79

Chapter 7
Storytelling **81**
Opening Statement: Telling Stories Ain't the Same as Lying 81
The Challenges of Telling a Good Story 82
Not Just Another "Case" 82
Stanislavski the Storyteller 85
Being Naked, Being Truthful 86
Connecting to the Audience 89
Adapting to Our Audience 89
Deciding on Your Characters 90
The Hero's Journey: Your Main Focus 90
Choose Your Own Adventure 92
The Five-Point Structure for Storytelling 93
Preparation 93
Closing Argument 95

Chapter 8
Now You're the Acting Coach: How to Prepare Your Witness .. **97**
Opening Statement: If You Train Them, You Will Win 97
Hollywood's Influence on Jurors 97
Eight Top Tips for Coaching Your Witness 99
Closing Argument 110

Chapter 9
Delivering Closing Arguments as Monologues 111
Opening Statement: An Attorney's Time to Shine 111
Concentration 112
Make It Personal 112
Sense Memory 113
So, How Can We Use Sense Memory in Our
    Closing Arguments? 113
How to Fine-Tune Your Sense Memory Skills 114
The Inner Monologue 115
Know Your Intention 116
Attitude 117
Faith or Fear? 119
Stage Fright 120
Obvious But Often Missed Questions to Ask Yourself 121
Closing Argument 123

Chapter 10
How to Take a Great Photo 125
Opening Statement 125
How to Pose for a Head Shot 126
How to Smile on Camera 126
Should I Try to Show My Personality in a Head Shot? 128
The Day of the Shoot 128
The Eyes Are Your Secret Weapon to a Great Head Shot 129
Ways to Keep the Eyes Alive: Inner Dialogue 130
Finding Actable Verbs 131
How to Pose for Group Photos 132
One Last Secret Tip 136
Closing Argument 136
Summation 137

Index 139

About the Author 146

Introduction

Why Acting Skills Are a Modern Attorney's Best Friend

The secret is out: The communication you send from your body is often more powerful than your words. You already know the law inside and out. You can research and write a brief that will stop district court judges in their tracks. Unfortunately, arguing that brief in court makes your knees sweat. Research and written communication is only half the battle for a modern attorney. Once the computer is turned off and the research is done, it's all about the performance—and you have been cast in the leading role. Lawyers who understand this and work hard to finely tune every aspect of their presentation skills will outshine opposing counsel, outperform their colleagues, and be compensated financially for their successes.

Why acting? Litigators are story tellers who must deliver the story with sufficient passion and energy to convince a judge or jury of the merits of their argument. From daily communications with your clients to the big case in court, public speaking skills *are* acting skills, and they are absolutely necessary to survive and prosper. When people watch and listen to you talk, do they describe you as "electric"? That is a sign you are doing a fabulous job. If they would describe your speaking style as competent, or even boring, you have a lot of work to do. Actors and attorneys share the same trials and triumphs of living in a world where clear communication rules and the weaker messenger cannot survive.

The good news is, this book will help you be yourself and use your own personality to succeed. Please note that this is very different from acting "naturally." Acting naturally for you may mean fiddling with your tie, spinning your wedding ring, saying "um" every other sentence, or talking so fast and muffled that no one can hear or understand you. Not only will an untrained performance cause you to lose the case, it will also lead to you getting pushed back on the list for a table at a fancy restaurant, or paying far too much for your bathroom renovation—all because of the signals you are sending unconsciously with your body and voice. Being yourself is freeing and powerful, and also extremely difficult. It is really hard to "just be yourself" when you are sitting in front of 200 people who are looking at you with expectant or cynical looks on their faces. If you don't have the passion and confidence to show your skills and abilities as a speaker, your message will still be delivered loud and clear. It just won't be the message you wanted to send.

Actors and attorneys share the same goal when they are in the spotlight—to be completely present in the moment, in a focused, authentic, and powerful way. Actors know the play, attorneys know the case. Are you bold enough to radiate passion and commitment with every word? To tell the story in a way no one else can? This book will teach you how.

I am not an attorney; I am a professional actor. I was paid to perform my first role at the age of 16, while my classmates were busy learning how to get high off spray paint. It was a lovely distraction from high school, to say the least. Then I married a lawyer and started watching attorneys perform at trial. My husband's friends started to ask me for advice, especially when they realized that their lack of confidence and skill in the courtroom was affecting their income. Then I started going to the courthouse in Chicago to watch the fascinating display of lawyers speaking and sharing information. I was shocked at what I saw. I guess I assumed that everyone just instinctively knew how to tell a great story, how to use their body in a nonverbal way to show emotions, and how to bring words off the page and make them an expression of thought. I was wrong. Since that time I have been working with attorneys and law firms across the country to help them achieve the presence and confidence required to speak publicly, whether in the courtroom, the conference room, or on the golf course.

I am being a little hard on lawyers here, I must admit. Sometimes lawyers are fantastic at getting in the spotlight and really taking control in a positive way. If you are one of those lawyers, this book is for you as well, because we can always be better, sharper, and more skilled. This book is for every type of attorney, because no matter what level you are at in your speaking ability, after reading this book you will have acquired more confidence, more tools to succeed, and perhaps may have a few laughs along the way.

Both actors and attorneys are expected to entertain, to inspire us to look at life a bit differently, and to share a story that has not been told. To do this, we need tools. We need to master our weaknesses and build on our strengths. We need to learn how to think on the fly. We also need to learn how to execute these skills on two hours of sleep. For most jobs, with only two hours of sleep you can most likely still go about your work routine and have a reasonably successful day. If an actor or attorney is not 150 percent on his or her game, it's immediately obvious to everyone, and the results are devastating. There are no "do overs," no second auditions, no practice trials. If you have bought this book, you already know the secret all actors know: You can never stop learning and growing if you want to be the best. Or if you want to get the best price you can on that condo in the Virgin Islands. Or if you just want to go to bed at night and say, "Wow, I really kicked some ass today." You can't ask for more than that, right? Let's go kick some ass.

Acknowledgments

This book is dedicated to Chad Mathis, husband attorney, and partner. This book would have never happened without you!

This book is the culmination of my life on stage, in the spotlight, and from working with attorneys across many states. My passion is to share the joy of creative expression and empowerment with others. I thank my parents and parents in law, Brian and Diane Mulhall and Mike and D'Nan Mathis, for their never-ending support; thanks to Flying Star for letting me loiter in their restaurant for days at a time as I wrote this book, and to the great people at ABA Publishing.

Special thanks to our amazing photo stars in this book, Jason Deshayes, Adrian De Windt, Lila De Windt, Frough Kamali, and Michael Youngman.

Chapter 1

The Art of Presence

Opening Statement: No One Will Listen If They Don't Know You're There

The concept of stage presence is a bit difficult to explain. It's like trying to explain love, sexual chemistry, or Lady Gaga. There are just no words that can really capture its essence. The French refer to it as having that "*je ne sais quoi.*" I would like to share with you a true story from my past regarding stage presence. It's about one of the only things I remember from high school, other than a vague sense of pain, embarrassment, and total misery. (I was a big nerd when I started high school, then I got contact lenses and my hair got less frizzy, but I'd be damned if I went out with any of those losers who called me a nerd. Too bad, suckers!)

In its truest essence, stage presence is a performer's ability to command the audience's attention through projection, focus, attention, expression, and confidence. In the case of rock stars, this involves fancy jumps and guitar smashing. No need to tip over the podium and kick the judge in the face, but somewhere in between that and being an indifferent lump of robotic information is what we will aim for.

Stage Presents

In high school, drama was not really considered cool. (I know, you're shocked.) Cheerleading was cool, student council was cool, and sports were cool. So the kids who loved drama were a tight-knit, fairly competitive group. By our senior year of high school, most of us planned to continue to study drama in college as a career.

One day, our teacher told us our assignment for the next week: Demonstrate what stage presence is in less than five minutes. That was all she said. We all quickly went home and devised our stage presence performance. For myself, I chose to come up on stage and tell a true story about the time my dad blew himself 20 feet across the backyard trying to light our barbeque. I used all my tricks to keep the audience hanging onto my every word, acting out the action of my dad flying across the yard with an oven mitt on one hand and a beer in the other. I felt like it went pretty well. Then Shawn Moon came up to perform.

Shawn Moon was my male counterpart—the boy version of me in the class. He was highly motivated, talented, and ready to work hard at his craft. When it was his turn to perform, he quietly snuck up on stage, and sat with anticipation in front of an imaginary medium-sized box that he was miming. He unwrapped this imaginary box with painfully careful moves, slowly pulling the ribbons off, carefully miming removing the tape so as to not rip the paper. The room was so quiet you could hear a pin drop. What the hell was in that damn box? After about four minutes, he finally got to the bottom of the wrapping paper, peeked into the box, and gently held out something in his palm. It almost seemed like it was glowing. He looked up at us, smiled, and waited for a beat. He slowly leaned forward, held up his palm, and said, "Stage presents!"

Damn that Shawn Moon! Stage presents/stage presence! It was brilliant and I hated him. The class exploded in applause and the teacher was scribbling away on her note pad, probably something like, "Well, Laura seemed like the real talent, but obviously Shawn has a much better grasp of stage presence, what a brilliant performer."

I think it is amazing that I can still remember that day, from so long ago, but I can't remember what I had for lunch yesterday. Stage presence can elevate your status as a public speaker immediately and demonstrate the true essence of what a great performer represents. Both attorneys and actors depend on incredible amounts of stage presence. Stage presence keeps the audience engaged, holds their attention, makes them believe in what you are saying, and in effect makes them give you the reaction you seek.

Self-Sabotage

There are many roadblocks when it comes to commanding stage presence. Let's go over how we sabotage ourselves:

1. *Lack of confidence.* If we believe we really know what we are talking about and have expressed ourselves as clearly and efficiently as possible, we glow with quiet confidence. A lack of confidence affects everything, from posture to breath control to being a bore.
2. *Being influenced by the room.* Sometimes the audience is difficult to master and control. They are hungry, confused, bored, or not giving you any sign of comprehension. This can cause an attorney to become self-conscious and nervous, and to doubt his or her speaking abilities. You have to remind yourself: I am the expert. I am in control of the entire experience that my audience or listeners are having.
3. *Not being ready for an emergency.* Assume that the laptop will crash, that the PowerPoint presentation will disappear, that four people will be slowly unwrapping candy, that you will get railroaded by opposing council, that you will be in a room that is very large and has an echo, or that the room is so brightly lit you feel like *you* are the one on trial.

This chapter will discuss all the ways we can prepare ourselves to battle our environment and our emotions in order to present the best self we possibly can to the public.

Developing Your Stage Presence

The entire concept of stage presence may feel like an abstract goal that is unnecessary. In reality, the quality of your stage presence will affect everything in your life. All the world's a stage, remember? Stage presence is more than what happens in the courtroom. It affects waiting for a table at the best restaurant in town, the toast you make at your brother's wedding, and how you tell your neighbor his dogs need to stop crapping on your lawn.

The more you explore your stage presence, both socially and at work, the more you become comfortable with truly being you, in the most effective and interesting way possible.

If you are having trouble finding a way to be yourself and still hold the room's interest, allow yourself to "play a role" while speaking in public. Some people have a sort of "alter ego" in court that is less inhibited than their normal personality. This concept of playing a role is what actors do for a living. If an actor is cast as a hippie from the '60s but in real life enjoys her Twitter account and shaving her armpits, she will take the time to research and become the character. She will base the character on the script, the time period, her imagination, and her sense of play. Dare I ask a lawyer to "play"? Will the world explode? Well, let's give it a try and see what happens. Attorneys are so often fixed on the facts, and on not letting the wrong thing slip out of their mouths, that a sense of play is the last thing on their minds.

The truth is, a sense of play leads to stage presence. A sense of play leads to people liking you, believing what you have to say, and, most important, listening to you. Really listening. If you can work toward completely revealing yourself in your performance and never holding back, you can suspend your fears of screwing up and let it all out. It sounds silly, but the best performers do just that. Once you have perfected your role through practicing the exercises in this book, just forget all the technicalities and instead utilize inspiration when you are in the spotlight. In both acting and improvisation, actors are taught all the rules and then told to throw them all away. Attorneys must do the same if they wish to have great presence in the courtroom, the conference room, and at the back table at the state bar convention.

It Isn't Natural

Stage presence is the quality that allows us to hold a very public position in a relaxed manner. We actors can eat lunch, get our hair and makeup touched up, and then sit in a room with 40 people and cameras a foot from our face, performing a scene where we cry at our mother's funeral. Without stage presence, imagination, and focus, we would never be able to maintain this relaxed state under such scrutiny.

For attorneys, the scrutiny is much more intense. Actors will have a director and the cameraman right in their face, but you will have everyone—the jury, witnesses, opposing council, your client, and your colleagues—staring you down and watching your every move. Stage presence allows us to remain ourselves under intense scrutiny from others. Attorneys with a high level of stage presence have a distinct advantage in a variety of professional and social situations.

The goal of stage presence is to be yourself—just a more relaxed, interesting, and focused you. Once you are free to be yourself, you are more relaxed and will carry less tension in your voice and body. Once the tension is gone, you are free to respond naturally to what is actually happening, using integrity and finely tuned reflexes. Perhaps one-on-one you are fantastic, but when you have an audience of 60 or more you lose your sense of control. You may start to speak quickly in a monotone or use a lot of vocal fillers, like "um," "ah," or "but-um." Maybe your face and neck tense up. Maybe you get sweaty palms and your voice is unsteady.

All of these psychosomatic responses to stress are going to affect the way people both listen and respond you. If the goal is that others listen to you and accept your message, this tell-tale sign of self-awareness will not help you achieve your goals. Attending a party, going to a networking event, taking a client out to lunch, and bumping into the judge at the supermarket are all opportunities to step up to the plate and expose ourselves (please don't take me literally).

Even if you have no desire to be the life of the party, Joe the Entertainer, or the guy who cracks everyone up with a great story or joke, we must be able to be relaxed enough to open ourselves up to the scrutiny of others, and be able to fully participate in life. Attorneys are storytellers, and, like actors, you have to make us believe yours is a story worth telling.

Developing stage presence is very much like running a marathon. If you jump in with no tricks or training under your belt, you may die. Okay, that was a bit dramatic, but haven't people died running marathons? The point is, if you want to run a marathon, you have to train. Let's begin our stage presence training by going over some simple exercises that will have you relaxed, confident, and showing your true self under pressure in no time.

Psychological Preparation

Take a minute to think about what really sabotages you when it comes to public speaking. Will a room of three or four people be comfortable for you while a room of 60 makes you sweat? Perhaps it's the exact opposite. Some people are fine speaking to a large, faceless crowd but clam up when speaking at a board meeting.

Perhaps for you it depends on to whom you are speaking. Will meeting with a potentially huge client send chills up your spine, but a deposition with a stranger seems very easy to do? Either way, you have perceived a threat somehow. So what is it specifically that is threatening? I can perform improvisation for children in a heartbeat, but when I perform for other improvisers it's easy to get self-conscious, because we all know the rules of the game. If I bend the rules and can't quite pull it off, I will be busted right away. This is a perceived threat.

> **Exercise 1.1: Telling a Joke**
> There are many websites that have jokes of every kind and even divide them into categories: kid jokes, religious, Canadian, clean, dirty, etc. Before the end of the day, make it a goal to find a joke that makes you laugh out loud. It is important that you laugh the first time you read it. If you don't laugh out loud, you won't have enough passion to deliver it with authentic flair. Then go the grocery store and say to the checkout clerk, "Hey, can I tell you a joke?" Here's your chance to test-drive the joke. If it works and he or she laughs, great! Now memorize a longer joke and tell it to your friends or co-workers. Work on your presence, passion, delivery, eye contact, and being yourself.
>
> Now, find a joke that is a bit longer. Maybe it takes one minute to tell. Memorize this joke and practice. Bring it up when having lunch with a friend or at a family dinner. The more you practice *initiating being put on the spot,* the easier it gets. A joke is a great way to break the ice. However, do not choose an x-rated joke for this experiment; try a clean

> joke or a joke everyone can relate to—a joke about mothers-in-law or taxes. You should love telling your joke, and people should love to hear you tell it. I really like the jokes on the *Prairie Home Companion* website; it's got lots of jokes for everyone.

Utilize a Sense of Calm to Develop Stage Presence

The previous exercise is a great way to get started because the stakes are low. Who cares if the lady at Walgreen's thinks your joke about the herpetologist and reptile dysfunction wasn't funny? Try again. Maybe saying "reptile dysfunction" is a bit intense for the average Joe while you are buying Oreos and moisturizer. Below is a quick tip for an instant sense of calm.

Quick Tip 1.1: Take a Bath

In order to acquire a sense of calm before speaking, the Bath Exercise is very easy to do, and can be done in under two minutes. This quick tip will help you gain a sense of calm and slow down your breath. You can do this exercise by sitting upright in a chair or your car, but not while you are driving! Close your eyes and imagine that you are immersed in hot water up to your neck, your head leaning on a bath pillow against the back of the tub. Start with the top of your neck, and work your way down your body. Try to feel the water moving over your skin, and the smoothness of the tub under you, supporting you. Feel the buoyancy that is keeping your arms and hands above water. Feel the heat forcing your breathing to slow down, the steam softening your face, your lips, and your entire body. Your breath becomes slow and deep. You can literally feel your heartbeat slowing down as your body relaxes. There is deep quiet except for the sounds of water moving around you. When you open your eyes, you will be relaxed, calm, and centered.

Visualization

When I was living in Austin, Texas, I had the pleasure of performing at "Esther's Follies," a famous stage show on 6th Street. Part magic show, part vaudeville, Esther's Follies takes no prisoners, offering biting, hilarious satire on all the news makers and events fit to parody. Part of my audition was to perform a magic trick that I was taught by the talented Ray Anderson, the magician at Esther's.

I managed to pull off the trick successfully at the audition and was cast in the show. On my first night, I was extremely nervous about getting to where I needed to be by the time the big reveal happened. Instead of panicking, I took the time in my dressing room to visualize how the magic trick would unfold, and I saw myself gracefully slipping into the perfect position at the perfect time. I saw in my mind the audience members' eyes wide with wonder, laughing, applauding, and whispering to one another, "How did she do that?" When the time came to perform the trick, it went perfectly, and I had a great first night alongside this talented cast of performers. Visualization works.

Athletes Do It Too

Creative visualization is the basic technique underlying *positive thinking* and is frequently used by athletes to enhance their performance. Before a big event, many athletes will take the time to visualize the execution of their entire experience, from start to finish. They feel the adrenaline in their body, and they see themselves performing flawlessly. If you don't fill your head with positive thoughts and images, your mind will jump in with all the worst-case scenarios. You will think about tripping, stuttering, how unprepared you are, how underqualified you are, and how nervous you are. So, what would you rather have running through your head?

When I coach actors for a big audition, I encourage them to see themselves performing their scene in a room of captivated casting directors and producers. I tell them to imagine the bigwigs smiling while writing things down in their book, like "This girl is perfect! We don't even need to keep auditioning the rest of the actors. We found what we were looking for!" When an actor does this, even if they don't get cast, they always tell me they had a great time at the audition. They say they felt relaxed and were happy with the performance they offered. As an actor, this is a good audition. As an attorney, this is building your reputation.

Visualization advocates suggest creating a detailed scheme of what one desires and then visualizing it over and over again with all of the senses (e.g., what do you see? What do you feel? What do you hear? What does it smell like?). Golfers may visualize the "perfect" stroke over and over again to mentally train muscle memory. While doing so they will imagine the feel of the club in their hands, the smell of freshly cut fairways, the sound of a beer can opening, and the sight of the ball sailing through the air and landing exactly where they were aiming.

In one of the most well-known studies on creative visualization in sports, Russian scientists compared four groups of Olympic athletes in terms of their training schedules:

- Group 1—100% physical training;
- Group 2—75% physical training with 25% mental training;
- Group 3—50% physical training with 50% mental training;
- Group 4—25% physical training with 75% mental training.

Group 4, with 75 percent of their time devoted to mental training, performed the best. The Soviets had discovered that mental images can act as a prelude to muscular impulses. Visualization practices are also a common technique in spiritual exercises. In Buddhism, complex visualizations are used to attain Buddhahood. Becoming enlightened is a cool benefit of visualization, but I would be happy with a great performance that gets me a role in a fantastic film. For attorneys, visualization helps in every aspect of public speaking, from one-on-one meetings with an important client to the day you argue in front of the state supreme court and a crowd of spectators. If it's good enough for Olympic athletes, it's good enough for us!

Can Stage Presence Really Be Learned?

Sometimes, as an acting teacher, I am asked if there are students that I just can't teach. They just can't act, and nothing I can do can help them. This is an interesting question, as the same query can be asked of stage presence. Can it really be learned, or is it something you either have or don't have?

Let's say I decided to learn how to play the ukulele (which is true). I have absolutely no musical ability (also very true). I have never played an instrument and I am a lefty to boot. So, after practicing a song for three weeks straight, I have become adequate at the ukulele and am quite proud to play "Hey Jude" for anyone who will sit and listen to it. My husband, a musician for many years, picked up my ukulele the first day I got it and just started playing a song. Just like that. He had never touched a ukulele before. Then I showed him the sheet music to "Hey Jude," and he was playing it perfectly in five minutes. What a show-off.

The point is, even though I may not be a great musician, I am better than I was three weeks ago, right? The goal is not to be perfect, it is to be the best we can be at whatever we challenge ourselves with. I know that anyone can learn stage presence. I have seen some of the most introverted attorneys walk into my studio, and after working with them on these techniques they walk away a confident public speaker.

The actor must perform the same play, often for weeks on end, but can repeatedly manufacture a sense of excitement and passion for the material even though they know how the story will end. A businessperson can walk into a room and sell his or her product or service as if it's the best thing since sliced bread, over and over and over. An attorney can argue passionately on behalf of his client, even when he knows his client has proven to be a lunatic and he can't wait to get rid of him. Is stage presence more natural for some people? Absolutely. But this does not mean that you can't learn how to make it look natural for you. It just takes practice.

My Killer Cat

In film acting, some of the most powerful demonstrations of stage presence occur when the actor is not saying a word. So how do performers like Al Pacino achieve such presence? How can we be drawn to a person who is saying nothing, not even moving? There are many ways of not moving. Watch your favorite actors in great movies and observe this phenomenon. An attorney in the courtroom may be still because her energy is gone. At the other extreme, she may be still yet poised, ready to spring. We can sense these differences because they matter—sometimes for our survival. If you can't tell when a predator is ready to pounce, then you're likely to be food quite soon.

Sometimes my cat gets a crazed look in his eye, and I know he is about to run over and bite my Achilles tendon. He's not moving, but I can feel the oncoming attack emanating from him. This evil attack usually happens as I am carrying a full glass of red wine over my beige carpet. I can tell the difference between him looking at me in his usual detached way and looking at me as he sees my delicious flesh slowly walk across the carpet. What type of message do you relay when you are not moving? Does your body display energy and passion, or do you go into standby mode? People are watching you all the time, especially when you are *not* talking or moving.

The Quickie Way to Obtain Stage Presence

Here are some quick ways to obtain stage presence without having to work at it:

1. Tequila shots
2. Hypnosis
3. Being struck by lightning
4. Hanging out with Axl Rose from Guns and Roses

If none of these seems plausible for you, let's go ahead and do the dirty work of actually practicing our stage presence.

Avoid Betraying Your True Self

Buddha said, "A lion would never betray his wife, but a Tiger Wood." (Sorry, I couldn't resist.) This exercise will help you tune into all the things that make you who you are. Offering personal tidbits about yourself can be a very valuable tool. Try to slip it into conversations with clients and checkout workers at the grocery store, and utilize it in public-speaking situations. I often bring a big color photo of my Saint Bernard puppy, Hoss, to my speaking events. Hoss is now two and a half years old, 200 pounds, and still growing. When people see pictures of Hoss and his giant head, they gasp and smile and coo. (They have no idea what it is really like living with a slobbering beast with a bottomless pit for a stomach, but we'll talk more about my husband later.) The point is, this picture of Hoss is a great ice-breaker. People will ask me six months after a presentation about how Hoss is doing. They remember! So, let's find things to talk about that show your true self.

> ### Exercise 1.2: Avoid Betraying Your True Self
>
> Think about the following areas of your life. We all have funny and interesting stories that can be pulled out when needed in social and professional situations. If you plan ahead by thinking of these stories before you're put in a situation where you are expected to say something about yourself, you will be in great shape. Otherwise, you may be left standing there looking like the highlight of your week is watching "Dancing with the Stars" with your mom. Some subjects might be:
>
>
>
> - Pets
> - Children
> - Travels
> - Sports you play
> - Musical instrument you can play
> - Favorite local restaurant
> - Dirt on your extended family
> - What you do for fun
> - Favorite TV shows or movies
> - Clubs you belong to
> - Where you went to school

The list goes on. Don't feel that you have to be someone else to be interesting. To explore who you really are, you have to think about all the details you can share to create a connection with your audience. If your life is super-boring, just start making stuff up—the crazier the better. Then make sure you do these things, and do them within the next six months so you don't get busted. One final note: Do your research and be sneaky.

Do Your Research/Be Sneaky

Before I meet new potential clients, I always read as much about them as possible from their Linked-in profile, Facebook, or their company website. In our conversation, I will slip in something like, "But you know, I lived in Chicago for three years, so I have no excuse to hate the cold." They will respond happily, "I lived in Chicago for three years too! How funny!" We will then chat about our favorite places to get deep-dish pizza, and a true connection is made. Likewise, if I am chatting with someone after an event, I will carefully observe her appearance. If I notice she has a napkin from a local restaurant in her purse, I will say, "Man, I'm starving, I could go for some enchiladas from Garcia's right now." She will state, "That is my favorite restaurant! I just had lunch there!" I genuinely like getting to know people; I just take chit-chat one step further by finding ways in advance that we might connect on a deeper level within seconds of meeting. In order to develop your public presence, you need to do the same.

Exercise 1.3: Entrances and Exits

One concrete goal that attorneys can work on is entrances and exits. The performance doesn't start when the first song begins; it starts when you enter the building. You shouldn't walk to your spot at the lectern like you're walking to pick out toothpaste at the grocery store. You should already be intriguing your audience. They should watch you and think, "Wow, I wonder what she's going to say." Remember Shawn Moon? The audience was captivated by what he was up to, and he didn't say a word until the last second of his presentation.

Something as simple as a graceful walk, shoulders back and chin up, can accomplish this. Taking a dance class will help you with this, or simply stick a note on your computer that says "Walk with Purpose!" Maybe tie an elastic band around your wrist to remind you for a week. Walk with a powerful attitude for your "role" . . . confident, heroic, strong, sexy, connected, expert, or anything else that makes you feel good.

Breaking Out of Your Shell

Finally, breaking out of your shell is one of the key elements to presence. True presence shows you are a leader, and that everyone should listen to what you have to say. As an example, imagine you have two employees. One is a quiet leader. He gets things done but never talks unless asked. He leads by example, which we've heard forever is a good thing, right? However, he avoids parties and social events at the office and is quiet in meetings. The other employee is a leader who is always part of every project and volunteers for everything, from helping you move your desk to putting up decorations for the holiday party. He always has a good joke and is a great listener. His presence is always felt at meetings, because he is always able to offer feedback and ideas. Who will most likely be moving up in terms of job offerings and opportunities at the office? If you fall into the first category, you need to break out of your shell in order to succeed, and show your presence as a leader.

Becoming an animated leader is a skill that most actors must master. If we don't have an air of confidence and entitlement when we walk in the door for an audition, the casting director can smell that lack of confidence a mile way. The fact is, it's a long day on a movie set. Directors want to work with people they like, who are easy to get along with, passionate, and easy to talk to. It's the same with attorneys. Will the jury choose the shy, quiet, sweaty, nervous attorney, or will they side with the attorney who has established a rapport and conveyed a sense of confidence and competence to the room? You may be legally correct in your arguments, but if you can't deliver them in a manner that conveys conviction and assurance, no one will listen.

Breaking out of your shell is more than your appearance in the courtroom; it also applies to small talk while entertaining clients or at work-related social events. At social events, most people grab a drink and hide in the corner. They talk to people they already knew before the event started. Small talk should be fun; it doesn't have to be boring, I swear. You just need the kind of passion that comes from standing on a chair.

Exercise 1.4: Standing on a Chair

In acting we talk of status—which character has high status and which has low status in a scene. For attorneys, playing high status is a valuable tool in the courtroom and the networking event.

Think of a story you can tell about your pets, a trip you took, the most scared you have ever been, why you hate camping, etc. Any story will do from your real life. Now, when you are alone, stand on a chair and tell this story to the room. Fill up the space, your voice traveling to every corner, your energy filling every inch of the room. Use hand gestures to help tell your story. This exercise is extremely freeing. It allows you to just do the damn thing and not worry about what others think of you. Let your voice be free! Break out of that shell you have put yourself in.

Closing Argument

At Esther's Follies, after the last show (it would be about midnight), all the actors were hungry for dinner. We would often go to a local Tex-Mex hole in the wall for chips and salsa and drinks. One of our co-performers, Andy, had a rock-solid Keanu Reeves impression. We would beg him to reenact Keanu Reeves moments while we were waiting for our food. We would squeal with laughter as he would walk halfway across the restaurant, run up to our table, look around with a dumb look on his face, and say "Whoa" in his best Keanu Reeves voice. We would call out scenarios for him to act out, like he walked in and saw his dog humping his sofa, or his bathroom was filled with cotton candy. He would do the exact same impression every time, making fun of Keanu's seemingly total inability to show emotion.

This was really funny to a group of actors. Even the patrons at other tables would start playing along and call out different emotions or situations for Keanu to fail at displaying. Andy never had any fear of making an ass of himself in these moments. To be clear, he was definitely making an ass of himself, but his lack of concern over it transformed him from an ass to the captivating center of attention in the room.

Actors are trained to be so expressive, in every way, for any reason, that the concept of not showing emotion was too funny for us. Do you see the irony here? You are far more likely to make a fool of yourself if you hold back, if you stay tight, if you don't take chances. For one day, practice really showing emotions. Tell stories and jokes with gusto. Start with the bank teller and work your way up to social events at work. People will start noticing you and listening to you. You will have command of the room simply by putting yourself out there. And this offering, this skill, this attitude shift, is stage presence.

Chapter 2

Vocal Variety and the Benefit of Keeping the Jury Awake

Opening Statement: You Can't Win if They Don't Listen

Just because an attorney knows what she is talking about, it doesn't mean her audience wants to listen to it. Techniques taught in this chapter will show an attorney how to easily transform vocal habits from the mundane to the expressive. By using techniques such as pointing, pace, volume, and tone, the modern litigator can utilize professional acting skills to convey an argument that will keep everyone interested.

We all know the pain of hearing ourselves on an answering machine or on television. The voice we hear bears little resemblance to the voice that is actually heard by other people (that's the good news!). The bad news is, most people have terrible vocal habits, and this absolutely will spill over from your personal life into your professional life. Let's review the most common vocal problems. Can you find yourself in this list anywhere? Don't worry: by the end of this chapter, you will be the master of your vocal presentation (I promise!).

1. Poor Diction

This is often caused by not being precise in thought or not carrying the thought through into the word. For many lawyers I coach, it also has to do with emotion in general. It seems that if too much emotion is revealed, a laser will come from the ceiling and zap you in the crotch. This does not happen. Really.

2. Overexplosive Consonants and Overemphatic Speech

This usually results from a lack of trust in your own ability to communicate, so you compensate by using harsh vocal technique and risk dipping into melodrama.

3. Losing the Ends of Words

This is also tied to not thinking through to the end of a thought. Again, this problem stems from a lack of trust in your ability to communicate.

4. A Stiff Jaw and Lack of Mobility in the Lips

This is often due to the development of bad habits, but it can also stem from a reluctance to communicate. Think of your wife or husband's boring family gatherings, and getting stuck in the corner talking to Uncle Wallace about how his tulip bulbs are looking especially healthy this year. That will make anyone clench their jaw, unless you happen to be a tulip enthusiast.

5. Clipped Vowels

Clipped vowels are caused in part by the fact that few people actually hear the music in speech. This is a big problem for many of the lawyers I work with. Too often lawyers will avoid committing themselves fully to the feeling, and they are afraid to show emotion. This keeps language at a down-to-earth, logical level. It can also sound robotic and heartless. Sometimes this is appropriate, but there are also times when language should sing.

6. Breathiness
Breathiness in vocal tone happens when you let the entire breath go out in a rush as you speak. This most often is caused by a lack of connection to the breath. For example, some people take one very shallow breath and use it to support an entire sentence. This can lead to the sentence fading into oblivion as the speaker runs out of breath.

7. Too Much Resonance
Too much resonance is a nice way of saying someone talks way too loud. Think of the loud guy at the fancy seafood restaurant that you can hear blab during your entire meal even though he is five tables away. This most often stems from a disconnection with one's surroundings. It can also be a sign that someone needs a hearing aid.

As actors, we are told to treat our voice as an instrument, practicing daily vocal exercises with the same discipline that a violinist practices scales and musical pieces in preparation for a performance. Guess what? Attorneys and actors share the same need: to keep their instrument in tune and ready to go. Your voice is the instrument by which you will carry the language of the argument (or play) to the back row of the courtroom (or theater). Attorneys are typically good about keeping their minds in top working order but often neglect to keep the conveyor of their accumulated knowledge in similar shape. This is like a quarterback studying a playbook night and day to understand an offense but failing to train his body to actually carry him onto the field and utilize the knowledge he has obtained.

How Loud Should I Be?

So, if we don't want to be the obnoxious loud guy at the seafood restaurant, how do we know how loud is too loud? There are three things to consider: 1) the size of the space you must fill, 2) the number of people you are addressing, and 3) the nature of what you are saying.

The goal of this chapter is to help you improve the flexibility of your vocal range, to aid projection without relying on microphones, and to improve the clarity of speech. These are skills you will use for the rest of your life, both in the office and socially. Let's get started.

Breathing

Simply put, your breath is the source of your vocal power and control. Most people spend all day taking "survival breaths." These breaths are shallow, in the chest, and take in just enough air so we don't tip over and pass out. Get ready for a mind-blowing high that doesn't involve Jack Daniel's, Red Bull, or hangovers. It's deep breathing! Think of the above list of common vocal habits we all may have faced: sentences dropping off before they end, breathy tone, nerves, and rushing. No matter the size of the audience, whether pitching a new strategic alliance with a local business or chatting with your dentist, breath control is the key to your success.

Exercise 2.1: Breathing Exercises

Exercise 1
First, let's make sure we understand what a real breath feels like. Lie on the ground on your back and put your hands on your belly, close to your belly button. Breathe through your mouth and feel the cold air run over your hard palate. Feel your stomach expand, rather than your lungs and chest. Your pants should get a little tighter with every breath because your stomach is expanding out. After about 10 of these breaths, you should feel like a million bucks (or at least not as likely to strangle your neighbor's barking dogs at 3 a.m.). Once you get a taste of real breathing, your life changes and everything gets easier.

Exercise 2
I am a huge fan of doing my vocal work in sneaky ways, since I have absolutely no free time to even unload the

dishwasher, let alone spend 20 minutes a day on vocal exercises. This is a great exercise to do in your car. Every time you are in the car at a red light, or on public transit, take time for deep, slow breathing that engages your diaphragm. You are literally retraining yourself how to breathe. Most people are subconsciously taught to use the stomach to help hold up the trunk of the body (think of how we might suck our gut in for pictures), and it doesn't want to free itself to become the expanding accordion that it needs to be.

Exercise 2.2: Opening the Throat

Now that we are actually breathing, we need to make sure the throat is open so that the sound can travel out of the throat and into the resonators. Here is a great exercise to do as you wait for your coffee to brew. Try it right now as a test run. Open your throat (good skill in case the law career falls apart and you decide to join the circus as a sword swallower). Put the tip of your tongue against the top of the back of your lower set of teeth. Stretch the middle of your tongue out thru both sets of teeth. Stretch the middle of your tongue out until you feel your tongue pull at its roots in the back of your mouth. Stretch and loosen those root muscles. Know where they are. Feel them relax after you have stretched them. If you can relax your tongue's root muscles, you can then open your throat, which will stop you from choking off sound. You will also stop swallowing sounds and getting them stuck in your soft palate.

Relaxation

To fully utilize the jaw, voice, breath, and tongue, your entire body has to be relaxed. For most people, as they approach the podium to speak, the stress is obvious. Their voice comes out as squeaky or weak, their throat dries up, and their knees are wobbly. If the body is loose, the speech can flow.

Exercise 2.3: Relaxation

To loosen tension in the jaw (as an actor with TMJ, I love this exercise), take the heels of your hands, rub them together to create warmth, and place them on your cheeks. Gently massage your jaw downward, away from its hinges. The jaw's hinges are just outside the opening of your ears. This also feels great if you are in the shower or bath because you can get your palms warm from the water before you place them on your cheeks.

To loosen the tongue, here is a great exercise that may have you drooling on yourself, but it feels great. Simply stick your tongue out as far as it will go and hold it out there (don't let it slip back) for 10 seconds. When 10 seconds are up, *slowly* let the tongue slide back into the mouth. It will now feel heavy and soft, sitting flat on the floor of your mouth.

Lamest Kiss cover band ever.

To loosen lips, as in the sinking of ships, I recommend utilizing your favorite type of alcohol. It works wonders on clients that are stingy with information and jurors who simply won't see things your way. It may not work so well with the ethics committee if you actually attempt that stunt.

Articulation

Articulation is the clarity of the formation of the consonant sounds using the organs of speech. These organs are the lips, tongue, teeth, and the hard and soft palate (the palate is the roof of your mouth).

If you are unsure of what you are saying or don't trust yourself, articulation is usually the first thing to go, but it's the most important. Teenage boys often articulate much less clearly when their voices begin to change. If they can't trust their voice to sustain the sound, it's safer (and less embarrassing) to mumble a bit.

Developing Articulation

There are many articulation exercises that you can practice during commercials of your favorite television show or while cooking dinner. The principle behind articulation work is to strengthen the muscles and contact points in the mouth that are used to form consonants. Once you find your own personal warm-up drills based on the exercises in this book, you can be ready and warmed up for any public speaking event in less than 10 minutes.

> **Exercise 2.4: Vowel Sound Warm-up**
>
> Take the following run of vowels learned in grade school: a, e, i, o, u. Now, pick any letter and place it in front of each vowel. So, you might say Ba, Be, Bi, Bo, Bu, or Ka, Ke, Ki, Ko, Ku. Really enjoy using your lips and breath to form the words. Ultimately this will help you discover your own strong and weak consonants, and you will never flub a word in a presentation again.

Tongue Twisters

I often write a few tongue twisters on an index card and try new ones every few days. It is really fun to get quite good at a certain tongue twister, ask your friends or co-workers if they can do it, and then dazzle them with how easily you can say it. After witnessing their inevitable failure, be sure to make fun of them and laugh at their attempts. Childish? Maybe. But I don't care. I take pleasure in the little things.

Tongue twisters are an excellent way to exercise an attorney's second most valuable tool, his speech. For many attorneys, their mind is their most valuable tool. However, we all know a few lawyers who are much better at talking their way out of trouble than they are at planning how to avoid it. This isn't a bad skill to have in your back pocket when you need it. The following exercise is a collection of tongue twisters to help prepare you for tackling tricky language when you have to think on your feet.

> **Exercise 2.5: Tongue Twisters**
>
> Say these phrases repeatedly, beginning slowly and working up to as fast as you can go. Tongue twisters will challenge your speaking skills and often lead to a few laughs as well. Here are my favorites. Try them all.
>
> 1. Three free thugs set three thugs free.
> 2. Black bug's blood.
> 3. A hot cup of coffee from a proper copper coffeepot.
> 4. Shining soldiers.
> 5. Toy boat.
> 6. Unique New York.
> 7. Red leather, yellow leather.
> 8. Irish wrist watch.
> 9. Budda Gudda.
> 10. Some shun sunshine, do you shun sunshine?
> 11. A critical cricket critic.
> 12. Peggy Babcock.
> 13. This is a zither.
> 14. Susie shall sew a sheet.
> 15. Truly rural.

Vocal Variety

Vocal variety allows us to express a wide array of emotions, interpretations, and color in our speech in order to reflect the true meaning of what we are saying. Without it, we sound like Ben Stein in *Ferris Beuller's Day Off*. There is nothing quite so disengaging as a monotone public speaker. When that speaker is an attorney attempting to convey a complex argument, a monotone voice can be a deadly weapon that induces a coma in everyone within earshot. Don't be that attorney. Let me offer you $30,000 in actors' vocal training in two pages. (I wish someone would have done this for me!) In this section, I will cover a number of areas that impact vocal variety, including rate, pause, inflection, pointing, volume, and pitch.

1. Rate

Most Lawyers who come to me complain that they speak too quickly, especially when they are nervous. When you talk too fast, you sacrifice articulation and emotional coloring of your words. Under pressure, you just want to survive and get the damn thing over with! But if you can't move your mouth clearly and quickly, you rapidly make complete nonsense out of the text.

So what's a lawyer who speaks too quickly to do? The good news is, talking fast is a bad habit, and habits can be broken. Remember that there are short silences between phrases and sentences. It's okay to stop when you hit a period. Give people time to absorb what you are saying. Before you speak, take a deep breath and concentrate on hearing the silence in the room. When you speak, exploit this silence. You are the boss! You are in charge!

There was a fabulous example of being comfortable with silence at a recent film festival here in Albuquerque, New Mexico, where I currently reside. The fabulous and talented Giancarlo Esposito (*Breaking Bad*, *Law & Order*, *The Usual Suspects*) was offering a free workshop in acting, and he had a packed house. I was thrilled! What would I learn from this immensely talented guy? I think everyone in the audience had very high expectations for this workshop. Yet after he was introduced he just sat in his chair, barefoot, and looked at us. No one said a word. He smiled. We smiled. There was silence for about five minutes, which is a really long time. It felt like we were part of a weird scientific experiment. Finally, he spoke and slowly said, "I'm really not sure why I'm here. I don't know anything that you all don't already know." There was a collective sigh of relief, and laughter. The pressure was gone for everyone. We relaxed, and so did Giancarlo. He used silence as a powerful tool to send a message. And we got the message, loud and clear.

2. Pause

If you are brave enough to dwell or linger for a moment, you have exploited one of the most effective ways of "marking a word" in order to give it particular importance. Hardly anyone uses pauses, maybe because it feels too egotistic to dramatically pause before a juicy word or bit of important information. I actually used pausing to get out of a speeding ticket—true story!

I was pulled over on a Friday afternoon on the way home from my studio. The police officer waved me over and asked me if I knew the speed limit. I said, sheepishly, "Thirtyish?" He sternly responded, "Thirty miles per hour, ma'am. Do you know how fast you were going?" I pulled my cutest look out and said, "Thirtyish"? It turns out it was more like fortyish. So, as he pulled out his notepad to issue my ticket, I said quickly, "Well, what if I was speeding for a really good reason?" He looked at me over his sunglasses and said, "Like what?" "Well," I said, taking a deep pause and stalling for time, "I'm starving?" He laughed, because he probably expected some lame excuse—but instead of getting an $80 speeding ticket, I left with a warning. Now, that's a good use of public speaking skills and pausing!

3. Inflection

Inflection is the rise and fall of the voice within a range of pitch. Inflection can provide a lot of color and energy to the voice. As a Canadian, I naturally use very little inflection. Irish people have lovely inflection, and impersonating the Irish accent is one of my favorite exercises for practicing inflection. When you are speaking, whether in a courtroom or in a client meeting, remember that you will convey your message much more clearly if you think about the rise and fall of your voice and make sure you do not speak with a flat monotone. If I can train the Canadian out of my voice, you can certainly add some inflection to yours.

4. Pointing

Pointing is a combination of inflection and pause. In general, there is one key word in every single sentence. The meaning of a sentence can be severely altered simply by choosing to point to a different word through inflection and pause. This is always part of an actor's preparation for a role in a play or movie. Actors understand that the art of acting rests largely on the power of pointing to clarify and enrich meaning.

As lawyers, you have to decide which words to highlight in order to convey your intended meaning. Great lawyers are able to think on their feet (as opposed to actors, who get to memorize the script in advance) and use certain "pointing" words to get the message across clearly. We do this all the time in daily conversations, but often in a public-speaking situation it all turns very monotone and boring. Virtually every sentence you utter has at least one or several words that you emphasize instinctively. The key is to keep those instincts alive when in a public-speaking arena. Remember, it isn't what you say but how you say it, and how emphatic you are.

> **Quick Tip 2.1: Understanding Pointing**
>
> Practicing the use of pointing will help you convey your message with much more impact and keep your listeners engaged. In the sentence "I called you last night," you can create different interpretations depending on the word you choose to point.
>
> 1. *I* (as opposed to someone else) called you last night.
> 2. I *called* (as opposed to e-mailed) you last night.
> 3. I called *you* (as opposed to someone else) last night.
> 4. I called you *last* (as opposed to tonight) night.
> 5. I called you last *night* (as opposed to in the morning).
>
> When you change the pointing word, you completely change the sentence.

5. Volume

Volume varies with the degree of support behind the voice (the energy of the breath) and the degree of resonance achieved. The wonderful thing about volume is that there are so many powerful ways to use it in public speaking, from a joking whisper to a bellow that fills the room.

The key is to understand when it is appropriate to either raise or lower one's voice. Speaking loudly can send a signal to the listener that you are making an important point, but it can also denote frustration or even anger. Speaking too softly will rarely get your message across, but there are key moments when lowering your voice can have a larger impact than raising it. Think about the message you want to convey. What emotion do you want the listener to walk away with?

6. Pitch

Pitch is simply the note of the voice. Newscasters use pitch to tell us how we should feel about each story. "An accident today caused three deaths after a fire in a local restaurant. In other news, the Albuquerque Isotopes are heading home to keep their three-game winning streak alive." A trained newscaster would never deliver these two sentences with the same pitch (although a sense of despair is common if you are a fan of the Isotopes. They're like the Cubs, only much, much worse). For both actors and lawyers, the most important pitch changes occur with a new thought, a shift of emotion, or when using an *internal character voice*.

To understand *internal character voice*, imagine a schoolteacher telling the story of *The Three Little Pigs*. She changes her voices so you know who is speaking. The more vocal variety the presenter achieves in pitch and emotional intensity, the more captivated you are by the story. Observe the wide variety of speech habits among your co-workers, family, friends, and even movie characters. Note how diverse speech patterns can be and how much more interesting a voice is when it is fully alive with color, energy, and variety.

The Care of a Lawyer's Voice

In theater school in Toronto, we were told that if we truly wanted to be professional actors, we had to take care of our voices. This meant no smoking, drinking alcohol, yelling, or poor sleep habits. This seemed outrageous to us. We were actors, after all! Smoking, drinking, and being generally loud and obnoxious were all we knew how to do and be! While some heeded this advice (lost touch with those folks), we generally acknowledged that, yes, our voice was part of the package, and it did need to be cared for. In case you wake up on the day of an important court date with a sore throat (which may or may not have anything to do with the fact that your college friend was in town, you went bar-hopping and ended up at a Snoop Dogg concert), here's how to rebound fast.

1) Gargle every hour with warm water and salt. The saltier the better. This is going to clean your vocal chords and throat. It also numbs them so you can get on with your life.

2) Drop the coffee and drink as much water as you possibly

can. Milk coats the throat and increases phlegm, so skip the milkshakes and lattes.
3) Drink a mixture of fresh lemon, honey, and hot water shortly before your presentation.

Remember the old adage: The show must go on!

Closing Argument

When you are preparing for a closing argument, developing questions for a witness, or even drafting a proposal for a potential client, you have to think about more than just the content. You also have to think about how you will deliver the content to achieve your goal. You can really draw a jury or judge in with the right preparation for your performance. And yes, it is a performance. Think about your rate, pause, inflection, pointing, volume, and pitch. Take notes where you would like your voice to rise and fall, and where you would like to pause. Highlight the words in each sentence that you would like to emphasize.

When you first begin to incorporate these techniques into your speaking, it may feel a bit garish or even comical. This is simply your ego and fear of looking foolish telling you to tone it down. As you improve on your speaking skills, you will come to realize that this is exactly how those engaging speakers you wish you could emulate sound. Playing it safe is simply boring when it comes to engaging others with our words.

Here's a final thought on vocal variety. People who speak well are considered better looking. It's true! So, what if speaking well also equated to making more money, being more relaxed in social situations, and generally succeeding in all areas of life? People who speak well are indeed blessed with all of these gifts, and now you can have them as well. More importantly, if you are comfortable with speaking in public settings, you will lead a much less stressful life. Attorneys already have a great deal of stress. They have to use their words every day in order to do their job.

Public speaking is the number-one fear for Americans. Most people assume that all attorneys are natural public speakers. We know this isn't actually the case. Why not unburden yourself by developing the presentation skills you need to succeed?

Chapter 3

Determine Your Character by Knowing Your Audience

Opening Statement: Know Yourself in Order to Be Yourself

If you think of your favorite actor or actress, they most likely are very good at playing a particular type of role. As a fan, you know they can play many different types of characters, but they are often "typecast" in a particular kind of role. The Rock (Dwayne Johnson) is the tough but lovable brute; Robin Williams is unstable, creative, and crazy; Al Pacino is always Al Pacino; and Paris Hilton . . . should never be cast in another movie again. Ever.

Attorneys each have a natural role as well. Some lawyers are very aggressive and dominate a room when they speak. Others are more thoughtful and bookish, and they tend to listen and react rather than try to control conversations. Some attorneys are naturally sympathetic and provide comfort for their clients, and some are very good at convincing a jury that they're just a simple lawyer looking at the problem with common sense.

It is important to recognize what kind of role you naturally play and develop it to its fullest. It is equally important to be able to switch gears when necessary and play other roles as well. The sympathetic attorney consoling her family law client in her office may need to turn into a snarling bulldog in the courtroom. Knowing which role to play, and when to play it, is crucial to your success as an attorney. It will allow you to present yourself in the best possible manner in any given situation. Just like actors have to develop different characters for different roles, attorneys have to develop their characters as well.

Actors know the value in being able to play a character in order to be believable, regardless of whether it is their natural type or not. There are methodical steps taken to make this happen. Each character should be well thought out, with precise body movement, a developed voice and inner dialogue, and a carefully crafted speech pattern. These are all combined to form a completely believable character.

So, where do we start? First, don't think I am trying to get you to be someone you're not. If you are 160 pounds with glasses, a small build, and a mellow demeanor, I am not going to ask you to you slam your fist on the table, bark at opposing council, or go off on a tangent, spitting saliva all over the jury. But you will need to develop a character that can be aggressive in a manner that suits your personality.

Feeling Like an Ass

To start, we have to get over the major hurdle I face with most lawyers when we practice the skills in this chapter. They feel silly, as if I am secretly taping them, and as soon as they leave I will post our session on YouTube for the world to laugh at them. (For the record, I will never do this, unless you tick me off.) Actors have skin that is tough as nails. The amount of rejection we face is tremendous. Actors often have to do very demeaning things for money to make ends meet, so my level of being humiliated is really warped. Lawyers can likely relate to this when they have to argue a client's position that they simply don't agree with and know it will make them look a bit foolish.

Perhaps my lowest moment as a young actor was when I dressed in a Giant Plush Teenage Mutant Ninja Turtle costume for children's birthday parties. The little angels would often gang up on me and all kick me in the crotch. Ha! My girl parts were impervious to their attacks. No one suspected a girl Teenage Mutant Ninja Turtle. I did, however, have to go home, take three painkillers, and drink a lot of red wine before I could shake off the terror of being a children's entertainer. So don't feel silly. Someone somewhere has already made a much bigger ass of themselves than you will ever be able to do.

You Have to Say It Out Loud

In order to practice the skills you are about to acquire, you must practice them out loud. Will it be hard? Maybe. But this is an emotional hurdle you have to get over. Here's the thing: Would you prefer to realize that your sentences are often supported by only one breath, and have no energy in them, safe at home in your bedroom? Or would you prefer to learn your mistakes in the courtroom, in front of peers, juries, and opposing counsel? Don't feel silly, feel prepared. This will add to your confidence in incredible ways.

You may feel self-conscious working through these exercises, but they are important in developing your technique. Don't worry, no one is watching.

Embrace What You Are!

Some people consider actors to be fake, artificial, and egotistical. I think they are just jealous and wish they were actors. Similar to actors, attorneys have to be able to "fake it" in the courtroom. You may be overworked, exhausted, stressed, worried, underprepared, intimidated, or just plain bored, but you *have to act like this is the most important thing in the world.*

An interesting phenomenon is that most people work on their public speaking skills only when they are speaking in public. Horrible idea! Do ballroom dancers only dance at competitions? Do football players run plays for the first time during the game? You need to practice, gain the skills, then go out there and knock people's socks off. Although we can improve our skills while putting them into action, the truly successful speaker prepares, practices, and prepares some more before going into action.

Knowing Your Audience

Knowing your audience is a true art form—similar to being a spy, or being able to cook Thanksgiving dinner and have it all hot and ready at the same time. It seems impossible.

When I perform improvisation, I often peek out at the audience before the show to see what types of hooligans I am dealing with. Is the audience mostly men, women, couples, kids, Eskimos? Are they quiet, conservative, rowdy, tired, bored, drunk? A drunken audience is a huge perk, as comedy is much funnier when the audience is drunk. However, this is much less likely to be the case for an attorney unless you are appearing before a judge with extremely poor control of his or her courtroom. This little peek at the audience allows me to analyze and shape how I communicate, how I relate to them, the characters I might play, or who I might pull up onto the stage as a volunteer. Let's apply this to your audience in the courtroom.

The Courtroom

If you take the time to look, you will see messages everywhere. Through the voir dire process, you already know a bit about your jurors' backgrounds. You can tell right away what type of jury you have based on numerous factors, including body language. For example:

- *How are they sitting?*—E.g., tall, proper, slouched, indifferent.
- *What are they wearing?*—E.g., high fashion, wrinkled, dated and worn clothing, covered with concrete spatter, covered with dog hair, covered with children's slobber, covered with their own slobber, jewelry.
- *How do their eyes look?*—E.g., glazed over, suspicious, overeager, soft, intimidated, power-hungry, distanced, thoughtful.
- *How are they holding their bodies?*—E.g., crossed arms, crossed legs, chin down in deference, chin up in defiance, overweight/underweight, avoiding eye contact, initiating eye contact.

So, you can use these little hints as you enter the room and as you address the jury. You can choose to mimic them or you can choose to complement who they are. Let's say the majority of your jury is blue-collar, middle-class, hardworking men and women. What type of approach do you think they would value most? I would try to make it real. Get to the point and be direct. Be an "everyman." Family is likely important to a group like this. They don't want to hear fancy legalese. They want the facts, and they want you to help them decide so they can get this over with and go home. If you show up in front of the jury all dramatic and fake, using big lawyerly words and barely making eye contact with them, they will not like you. If they don't like you, they won't like your story. Adopt an earnest tone and speak to them professionally. Most attorneys do not come from a family of professionals. This shouldn't be difficult.

Each time you begin a new thought, it's an opportunity to do more research on your audience, and see how they are responding to you. Don't say things that aren't true. We normal people hate that. Here are some examples of starting sentences that are not true:

1. *"This case is very cut and dried."* Really? Then why are we all here?
2. *"Members of the jury, right now you are trying to understand all the facts."* No kidding, Sherlock.
3. *"Mrs. Murphy, how are you today?"* You really don't care how she is, so don't ask her.
4. *"I've just got a couple of questions for you."* Yeah, right. This is never true.

Instead, start off strong! Bold! Provide information, and then see how the jury responds. Try something like, *"Dr. Lush, isn't it true that the day you performed surgery on Frank Muller you were under the influence of alcohol?"* Great question. The jury will be all ears to hear how the good doctor responds to that one. True, not every opening sentence can be that bold, but at least get in there with passion and get the jury interested in the questions you ask from the beginning. When addressing the jury directly, the "shock and awe" approach, as I like to refer to this technique, can work wonders. Just remember to start bold. I'm sure you have heard before that people only remember the first and last thing you say. Well, it's true. Remember it, love it, live it.

Another way to grab their attention is for you to sound truly interested in what you are saying. This is where the acting comes in. So *act!* You've reviewed the facts of the case a thousand times, prepared every brief and motion (you would never pawn that off on associates, would you?), and rehearsed your opening argument or closing a million times. Well, guess what? The jury or judge has never heard (at least out loud) what you're about to say.

Pretend this is a fabulous Hollywood movie directed by your pal Steven (Spielberg) and you are the lead actor. This is your big scene. Use enthusiasm and energy in your voice, and your body should match this as well. Your eyes should sparkle with interest and vitality. Think of yourself as intriguing, bold, fascinating, and edgy. If you think of yourself this way, so will everyone else. I promise, it works like a charm every time. This also applies to dating, but that is a different book.

Obviously, overt histrionics in the courtroom are not likely to fly with too many judges. Nonetheless, you can take control of the room and are more likely to be listened to if you are willing to add a bit of character to your presentation. No one enjoys being bored, and let's be honest—court proceedings are all too often a snooze fest.

The Audience Has Left the Building

So what is a litigator to do if you are working hard at being passionate and intriguing, and you see jurors number four and nine waft away? Their eyes glaze over, and you see them mentally placing their Papa John's Pizza order in their mind? First, don't take it personally. This is comparable in acting to when an audience member leaves at intermission or, even worse, in the middle of the play. People's brains can only handle so much before they blow a fuse and start to wander. Here are some ways to wake them up from their coma:

1. Raise your voice on key words.
2. Use a bold movement, like stepping toward them, spinning, or freezing.

3. Not saying anything for a moment in a pregnant pause of anticipation.
4. Laugh or chuckle at what was just said.
5. Exhale loudly before an important observation or question.
6. Stop, smile, and walk slowly toward the jury as if you are all sharing a secret.
7. Slap your paper on the desk and quickly move to the front of the courtroom, as if a huge revelation has just occurred.

When in doubt, just ask yourself, "What would Al Pacino do to get a jury's attention?" Now dial it back about two notches. Really, this works. He is a bad-ass, and so are you. You just have to claim the floor. Spielberg wants to get this scene in one take; there is no tomorrow. Let's do this right the first time so you have no regrets at happy hour.

Determining Your Character

Now that we know how to analyze, talk to, and engage the jury, it is time to determine what type of character you should play depending on the case. Don't be fooled: This character work is basically choosing an attitude, and all attorneys need to be able to slip on an attitude at a minute's notice. It is a tactical choice, born of necessity and proactive logical choices to get you what you want. The "script" of every case will be different, with different "characters" and "plot developments." It is up to you to determine what your role in a case will be. Will you be the pushover who hands opposing counsel the case on a platter, or will you be the hero who wows everyone with your presence, intelligence, and charisma?

When questioning your client on the stand or speaking to the judge, it is pretty safe to have a friendly or congenial attitude. If you want the jury to like your client, why talk to him like your teenage daughter who snuck back into the house at 2 a.m., smelling like smoke and peach schnapps? I know that attorneys want to kill their clients half the time (don't forget, I'm married to one of you people), but save that for when the case is over and you have received your full fee. Using inflection, tone of voice, and attitude, we can alter our persona to suit our needs.

40 CHAPTER 3

[SMUG] [CYNICAL]

[JOVIAL] [SYMPATHETIC]

So here is a cheat sheet for deciding on your "character."

1. When speaking to a client or witness, try using a character that is:
   - friendly
   - interested
   - engaged

- curious
- polite

2. When dealing with a cross-examination of a witness who is not being truthful or is evading your questions, try using a character that is:
   - condescending
   - cynical
   - incredulous
   - outraged
   - sarcastic
   - surprised

3. When trying to arouse sympathy for your client's story, try using a character that is:
   - compassionate
   - friendly
   - hopeful
   - sympathetic
   - understanding

4. When showing that you have succeeded in proving your point and the case is a no-brainer, try using a character that is:
   - emphatic
   - excited
   - happy
   - hopeful

These attitudes are a key factor in using a logical and specific tactic to get what you want. You and I know that you will be faking it most of the time. Because of this, it is crucial that you practice how to act out these emotions before you are put on the spot. If you don't have an attitude behind your words, I can tell right away. Attorneys will often come across as detached, bored, neutral, mechanical, or just plain robotic when we first begin working together. Do you really care about what you are arguing? I have no idea. Can you *act* like you care? Absolutely! So, pick an attitude and change it accordingly as you read the audience, using the jury's body language, posture, eye contact, and the nature of the case to help you make the appropriate choice.

Applying Your Voice to the Chosen Attitude

You may be thinking that no matter what attitude you have chosen, they all seem to sound or feel the same. If this is happening, I suggest that you explore the concept of using your breath to explore your character and choices. If you were to read a screenplay of one of your favorite movies, you would be very impressed with how the actor breathed life into the character, the script, and the mood of the film. Actors take the one-dimensional character on paper and give it a life, a voice, a soul. When you have an opportunity, pick up a screenplay for a film you have seen. Think about how you read the words on the page and compare it to how the actors performed it on screen. It sounds very different, doesn't it? When actors read parts, they see themselves in their minds as the character. A key element to this exploration is the breath.

As you deepen your skills and master these concepts, your breath, which allows you to make sounds and eventually use your voice, is the beginning of the recognition of the impulses that are being released from within. It all starts with the breath.

Achieving the relaxation and concentration needed to play a character is a huge task, but one that can be can be conquered if you take the time to first center your breath. Don't worry about feeling like a big hippie, sitting in your office breathing. This stuff will honestly change your life, both professionally and personally.

> **Exercise 3.1: Applying Your Voice to the Chosen Attitude**
>
> Pick an attitude or character you want to play. Place all your concentration on your breathing. Allow your thoughts, images, and feelings to flow through your breath, slowly and easily. If you feel yourself spacing out, just gently bring your attention back to the present moment and your breath. After about 10 minutes, start asking questions of your imaginary witness in an attitude that is joyful, confused, concerned, or whatever best represents your chosen character. Repeat this with other attitudes in order to explore all the types of characters you can play.

Creating Relationships

The final piece in the puzzle of determining your character by knowing your audience is creating relationships. Our goal is to create a relationship with the jury, judge, or whoever your audience may be. Did you know that in films, you may show up on a set for the first time, meet your "film wife" or "film husband," and then shoot a scene where you are at his or her funeral, or, even worse, a sex scene? You just met this person! How are you supposed to cry real tears of mourning, or get naked with 40 crew members five feet away, when all you have said to them is "These cinnamon rolls are really great, have you tried them?" The point is, each actor has to create a relationship with the environment and other characters though his or her imagination, *before the big day*. It's the same for attorneys.

Ask yourself, what is the relationship I want with the jury? Do you want to be:

- the big brother, protective and knowing?
- the best friend, honest and real?
- the law enforcement officer, offering rules and matter-of-fact information?

- the mother, caring and aware of feelings?
- the mischievous college friend, fun-loving and straightforward?

Some jurors like to be coddled, some like to feel they are the all-knowing masters of the universe, and some just like to be told how they feel about the case. I find the best relationship with the jury is somewhere between a best friend and the no-bull college buddy—honest, high-energy, intriguing, and enthusiastic.

When you have a relationship with the jury, they can feel it. You look at them differently, you smile differently, and you connect in a more real way, as opposed to a perfunctory or mechanical relationship. Who knows, you may get so good at creating relationships that you don't even need to read the jury, *because you are creating the exact mood and relationship that YOU want, to best serve your case.*

Closing Argument

The thrill of performing is something magical, and I will most likely be onstage or on a set until the day I die, or at least until they drag me off. If it is not fun, *make it fun.* Play Matthew McConaughey with 10 pounds of rare jewels stuffed down your very small Speedo. Or play Angelina Jolie, knowingly moving through the room with quiet dominance. You can even play William Shatner's "Denny Crane" character from "Boston Legal," oozing confidence while appearing slightly addled. Find the character traits and body language that will best serve the needs of your client by delivering their message most effectively. The attorney who can master this skill is an attorney who is going to win a lot of cases.

Attorneys, the curtain is rising. Which character will you play today?

Chapter 4

Being in Your Body

Opening Statement: Effective Speech Delivery Involves the Whole Person

Being "in your body" is important. Did you know that over 70 percent of your message is not what you say but how you say it? Body language accounts for 70 percent of our understanding of emotions, our reception of subliminal messages, and our grasp of relationships. This is fascinating stuff. You may prepare the ultimate opening statement or closing argument for your case, and your body language may convey an entirely different message than the one coming out of your mouth. It is important that your body lines up with exactly what your words are meant to convey.

Most of the time, the attorneys I work with place themselves in a tiny little box when they speak, never allowing themselves to communicate more than half an arm's length out in any direction. When I encourage them to loosen up and use their body to express themselves, they try the exercise again and barely get any air under their armpits or move more than an inch. They know they have not done what I asked. For many attorneys, this feels weird, extravagant, or even flamboyant. They have been taught to stand firm behind the lectern and keep hand gestures to a minimum. They feel that if they move too much they will come across like Jack Nicholson on an alcohol-fueled bender. But guess what? As an attorney you are a storyteller, just like actors.

Your ability to communicate affects your success in both work and personal relationships, so let's figure out how to move our bodies without feeling like a dancing monkey.

The Neutral Position

An important step for both actors and attorneys is the development of the neutral position. It is surprisingly difficult to consciously place ourselves in a neutral state. When speaking in public, or even in one-on-one conversations, we do not realize when our fingers slide along pant pockets or fiddle with a pen or change in our pocket, or we sway back and forth as if we are on a boat. "Neutral" is defined as being "neither one thing nor the other." Once you have the neutral state as a skill, you can automatically get rid of tensions, mannerisms, and personal quirks.

The neutral position is all about gaining control of the image you convey to those around you. When we can be neutral, we can build positive body habits and messages from a clean slate, as opposed to whatever unconsciously happens when we are in front of a roomful of people. Would you rather have complete control or leave it up to your stress level and unconscious movements? We can harness the power of body language to get a hot date, receive a big promotion, land a huge client, and get out of speeding tickets. Things that once seemed extremely difficult or even impossible are now fully in your control.

How Do You Know You Are in a Solid Neutral Position?

In the neutral position, your posture is relaxed but strong. Your head should be on the same vertical plane as your spine. Stop sticking your head out like a turtle. You! Right now! Slide it back. Bring the book or computer to *you*. Better, right? Now do this all day. Good posture helps you breathe properly and project your voice effectively. It will also make your mother proud of you the next time you visit, and that alone may be worth all the trouble.

Quick Tip 4.1: The Neutral Position String Pull

Before you speak, imagine a string pulling up from two places—the first place is from the middle of your head up to the sky and the second string is from the middle of your chest, across the room up to an angle.

When you stand still, be careful not to sway or rock. Imagine there are deep roots, like a tree, coming from the bottoms of your feet that secure you to the ground. Think about how great it is to have the ground to support you; enjoy the feeling of the floor under your feet. Make sure your shoulders are square. Do not lean, slouch, or hunch over when you walk. Stand tall! Pull the string up! Be proud of yourself—you have an important message to communicate.

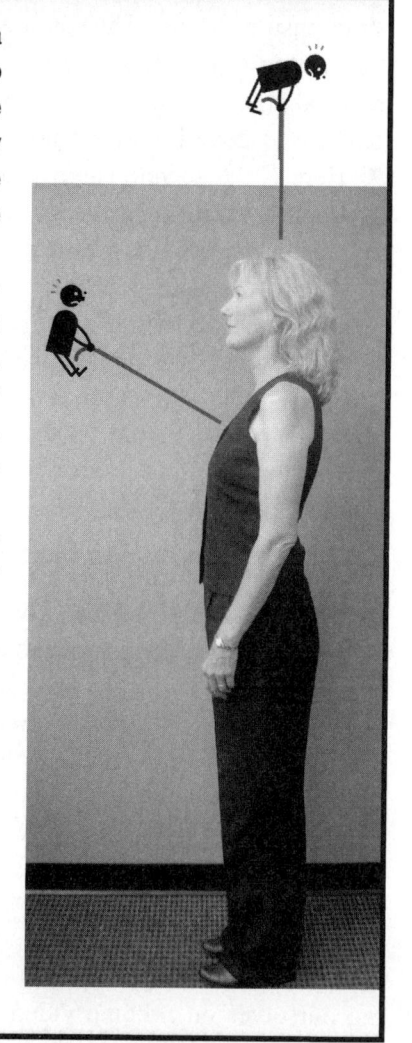

Some of the worst advice for people about to engage in public speaking is to "be natural," or "be yourself." This is terrible advice. What if it is natural for you to chew your lips when you talk, or sniffle, or say "umm . . . ", or hunch over? Does it look natural to the audience? No! It is distracting for the listener and completely devalues the meaning of the words being spoken. These little quirks can convey a message to your audience that you do not intend.

Perhaps you clench your fists when you talk. This may be normal for you, but your audience interprets it as nerves, inexperience, being unsure, or just that you are an uptight person. What messages are you sending? You may have a complete grasp of the subject material, but those late hours you spent preparing questions for tomorrow's deposition have now left your hands shaking like a leaf.

Here is the secret: There is a wonderful and vital personal freedom and confidence in becoming one with the space around you. If your hands feel like weird pieces of clay that everyone is staring at when you speak, you have simply not taken possession of your personal space. Children take possession of their personal space all the time. Infants will joyfully and without notice slip their feet right into their mouths if they so desire. When is the last time you put your foot in your mouth? I will resist a lawyer joke here and move forward.

Remember: An Action Is Stronger Than a Word

Do you watch television? YouTube? Home videos? What about Skype? As human beings of the twenty-first century, we rely heavily on our sense of sight. As presenters of important material, attorneys have to be able to show an understanding of the material at hand not only with words but with their body language.

"Do You Think I'm Sexy?"

Besides being one of my favorites to play at biker bars, this Rod Stewart song is a great lead-in to our first exercise. We are our own worst critic. Hearing ourselves on an answering machine or watching ourselves on a home video makes us recoil in horror. But you can convince others to feel a certain way about you based on you how you feel, or at least how you convince yourself that you feel.

This exercise may bring up strange emotions. We have far more "Ugliest Creature" moments in our lives than "Most Confident Person in the World" moments. But do you feel the changes both internally and externally? It is mind-boggling how a simple change in perception can actually make you *feel* different. You do not have to say a word for others to know whether you consider yourself the

> ### Quick Tip 4.1: "Do You Think I'm Sexy?"
>
> Imagine you are standing in front a full-length mirror and you see your reflection as the Most Confident Attorney in the World. Take a moment to preen, flex, and turn, to see what you are wearing, and to admire yourself from all possible angles.
>
> Now, step through the mirror, and as you do, you will become the Ugliest Creature in the World. Examine how you have changed, what you are wearing, and allow yourself to explore every distortion in your appearance.

Ugly Creature or the Most Confident. This internal impression changes our breath, our face, our posture, and our overall body attitude.

Just for fun this week, enter every room, every restaurant, and every hallway as the Most Confident Person in the World. Once you can do this automatically, your presentation will go 10 times better than if you do not do this exercise at all. Try it, and e-mail me what happens.

Body Language: What Is the Story You Are Telling?

Body language is really a key to people's emotions and moods. These can be interpreted by watching facial expressions, tensions or freedom in an individual's body, closeness or distance between others, eye focus, and energy level. The attorney with the most control over her body language is the attorney most likely to control the situation and convey her message as she intend it to be conveyed. This applies to the courtroom, the conference room, and even the bedroom. The following exercises and tips are designed to assist attorneys in gaining control of their bodies.

Exercise 4.1: Observation

On a free day (call in sick if you never have a free day), wander around a shopping mall, airport, or public building and see how many assumptions you can make about people you observe. Arrogant? Stupid? Confident? Stoned? Weak? Powerful? We have to look beyond the things we see in an attempt to discern the real intention behind people's actions. What messages are they sending through their body language? Do these messages truly represent how these people wish to be perceived? Take notes of the body language you see in people who have traits you wish to convey.

Another great observational exercise occurs at restaurants. The next time you are at a restaurant, determine the relationship between two people at another table just by discreetly watching how they use their bodies to express themselves: their physical positions, use of the chair, gestures, facial expressions, degree of energy or animation, the space between them, method of eating and drinking, the changes (or lack of changes) that occur when the waiter appears, and their eye contact. Again, take notes.

The next step is to jot down what message you think your body language conveys. What traits did you see in others that you would like to convey yourself? By observing others, we can learn what behavior we would like to see in ourselves. This is the path to successful communication.

Equally fascinating are the messages that we *do not* want to send. If you have dry eyes and constantly blink, it may seem that you are saying, "Damn, this person is boring—I have to wake up!" I personally tend to purse my lips when I am thinking. I may look frustrated or like I am suppressing feedback when a client is providing me with information about his latest idea or conflict. This nonverbal message may cause him to become self-conscious, or to stop offering his opinion to me based on his assumption that I hate what he has to say.

Do you crack your knuckles? What message does this send? I have witnessed an attorney absolutely annihilated by a judge for cracking his knuckles while the judge was speaking. There is nothing worse for a communicator than to lose control of her body in stressful situations. So, what messages do *you* send in meetings or when speaking to others? How are you sitting right now? What part of you is tense or locked? Are your eyebrows low or furrowed? Is your jaw locked? These body tics most likely happen when you are listening as well. Gaining awareness of these subconscious actions is the first step toward controlling the message your body is communicating to others.

How to Act Like a Tough Guy

A great exercise we often warmed up with at Second City in Chicago is leading with different parts of our body. If you were asked to walk like a "tough guy" you would probably do the same thing most people would do: puff out your chest and raise your chin high. These actions are immediately recognizable as bravado and an intention to convey a certain energy to anyone watching. This energy flows outward into a new form through your actions, and you begin to experience yourself anew. It extends you further from your "ordinary" self, and it summons new energies inside you. The value for attorneys in acquiring this skill is that it allows all your human energies to be accessible and controllable in the process of creation.

If you have done a great job in presenting an argument and are coming to the end of your presentation, your body may be communicating that you have failed miserably due to the hard work you have just put in. In your mind you just kicked some butt, but you're body is screaming, "I'm exhausted!" If you appear disappointed, everyone else will also be disappointed in you and your message. You should be able to slip into a confident or optimistic body language in seconds to continue to send home the message.

So, when no one is home, let's practice using body language to show a type of "character" or attitude you may choose to play in order to better tell your story.

Exercise 4.2: Leading with Your Body

Walk around the room, and lead with different parts of your body (chin, chest, toes, elbows, nose, arms) to convey the following attitudes: angry, condescending, cynical, deflated, empathetic, excited, friendly, hopeful, incredulous, outraged, parental, sarcastic, surprised, understanding. This is a really fun exercise, as it allows you to explore the many ways you can tell your story with saying a word.

When you discover how to convey an attitude without speaking a word, you're one step closer to presenting an argument that will be hard to ignore. Imagine how powerful your words will be when they are combined with body language purposely intended to convey a particular attitude or emotion!

Gestures, or "Why Are My Arms So Long?"

Actors don't worry about things like gestures. We just make sure that our body matches our words. Attorneys should do the same. This is much more natural than learning fancy gestures that have you looking as if you trained at the Bill Clinton School for Thumb Pointing.

Your body is a reflection of your personality, and here is a chance to show what makes you unique. A book on gestures may have you doing something that will never feel comfortable to you. Here are five guidelines to find your own way to express yourself nonverbally.

1. Suit the action to the word and occasion. Be decisive. Make gestures purposeful and reflective of what you want to say. Bang the table when you want attention. Bring your fingertips together when making a point you really want your audience to focus on and understand. Don't be boring; take chances, and you will have people eating out of the palm of your hand.
2. Just respond naturally to what you think, feel, and see. It is natural to gesture; we do it all day. Remember the people you were watching at the airport and restaurants? They gestured the whole time and never thought about it for a second. Think about what gestures are natural for you and whether they line up with what you wish to communicate.
3. Don't overdo the gestures. You are not an itinerant preacher on a cross-country tour. Find a way to be neutral until a gesture naturally comes out of you. Putting your hands in your pockets does not count as neutral. Or on the lectern. Or messing with a pen. Try just loosely clasping your hands in front of your belly button, with a bit of space under the armpits, so you don't look like you're being held hostage. This is a great neutral hand position. If you happen to be larger, or pregnant, keep your hands at your side. Placing them on top of your belly may look more like you are resting your arms on your stomach than anything else. Convenient for you, distracting for your audience.

4. Match your face to the gesture. If you call out "Yes! That is exactly my point!" and your hand curls into a powerful punch, but your face looks like you have been watching a documentary of the history of soap, the message will not make sense. If you are conveying excitement about a point in your speech, show it in your face with a big smile.
5. As we now know, it is a fact that people who are well spoken are considered better looking than those who are not successful at public speaking. Nice! People are looking at you right now thinking how dead sexy you are. Does that make it more fun and easy to be yourself? Just hold the "come hither" winks for happy hour.

Eye Contact

Last but not least, we need to discuss eye contact as a vital part of body language. Eighty percent of nonverbal communication takes place with our face and eyes (or, in the case of Barack Obama or H. Ross Perot, with their giant ears).

Eye contact is cement. It is glue. It is the secret ingredient that makes people listen to you, trust you, and care about what you have to say. So, how do you find the balance between trying to make eye contact with a roomful of people and staring in a creepy, desperate way at the lady in the front row who reminds you of your sweet Aunt Linda? Here are the tips used by actors who perform for audiences of one and audiences of thousands.

1. Know what you're talking about. If an actor has not worked on her audition or role, the performance is crap. This holds true for attorneys as well. Know the material backwards and forwards. If you lose your notes, or the PowerPoint presen-

tation freezes, you will not be caught looking like a fool because you know the information. You have the confidence to continue without becoming flustered.
2. During auditions for both theatre and film, casting directors hate it when you look at them. It really creeps them out. I guess it makes sense. I would not want some crazy actor in my face, screaming, "Why? Why, Momma? Why did you leave me and Billy when we were babies?" Select one person and look at him or her until you have finished your sentence or thought. Then switch your gaze slowly to a new person. If you are in a very large group, look at chunks of two or three people at a time. You want everyone to feel like you are talking directly to them. This makes the listener feel good. To be on the safe side, when a judge is speaking to you, you'd better look her directly in the eye.
3. Take a temperature check and see if the audience or jury is with you. What do you see? If they look bored, there could be many reasons other than the fact that your presentation or argument is boring. Maybe they cannot hear you. Make sure the microphone is working or, if you are in an environment without a microphone, raise your voice.
4. Does your audience or jury look puzzled? Repeat, rephrase, or slow down. Ask them if they are with you (although I don't recommend asking a judge if he is following your argument). Be ready for them to say they are not. Calmly rephrase your last thought and keep checking for comprehension.
5. If your audience or jury is truly bored, use humor, vocal variety, or a powerful gesture or movement to wake them up.

Closing Argument

As human beings of the twenty-first century, we rely heavily on our sense of sight. As presenters of important material, attorneys have to be able to show their audience that they understand the material at hand not only with words, but with their body and body language.

By now you should be aware of the message your body is sending. If you're having trouble with self-analysis, ask a colleague or friend for help. Just be prepared to hear things that you may not like. The next step is to make sure you are making the best choices possible to help tell the story in the most effective nonverbal way you can. So, get your sexy self in front of the room and tell your story on your terms and in your own way.

Chapter 5

Taking Depositions/ Being a Talk Show Host

Opening Statement: You're Exactly Like Larry King

Tim Russert, Oprah Winfrey, David Letterman, Howard Stern, Larry King. What quality interviewers have in common with one another is marrying the gift of gab with the ability to glean juicy details from their guests. There are many parallels between interviewing and taking a deposition. The end goal is to get the person you are talking with to respond to you and share information he or she never anticipated sharing. In this chapter we will explore the tricks of the interviewing trade and learn to use them in depositions.

The first step for most actors who are tired of starving and want a full-time paying gig is to film or record a live performance to showcase their on-air experience and ability to interact confidently with guests. Whenever I pull out the video camera during private sessions with lawyers, I can feel them cringing before I even remove the lens cap. This is because the camera does not lie. It can tell whether you are actually listening versus just glazing over and waiting for your turn to speak. Even worse, it will catch you speaking nonstop and never allowing your interviewee to truly respond to your questions. This is tricky stuff. Oprah Winfrey and David Letterman make it look easy, but this gift of gab is a finely tuned skill that every litigator must be able to pull out and apply during a deposition. Obviously, the conditions of a deposition are much more serious than that of a celebrity interview on a late-night talk show. Nonetheless, a good talk show host has a knack for pulling information out of his guest that an attorney can use to her advantage.

Some of the skills needed for a great deposition are also covered in this book in other chapters. Being able to cultivate mental and verbal flexibility and the ability to ad-lib if necessary are very important. Although you are in control of the questioning, you never know when the deposed will say something that takes you down an entirely different track from the one you set out upon.

Depositions in General

Taking a deposition can be an exciting experience for a lawyer, despite the fact that most depositions are not really that glamorous. It's just you, the deposed, opposing counsel, and a court reporter or two. You should, of course, review all the rules regarding depositions if you're not completely comfortable with the procedure. Achieving mastery of the rules of your profession is something I leave to you. I'm here to teach you how to take these rules and publicly demonstrate them in the most powerful manner possible. Let's review the various purposes of depositions.

1. This is your opportunity to learn the witness's version of the events. Depositions allow one side to find out what a witness or a party knows about the case. This helps you in your strategy for trial.
2. The deposition fixes a witness's account so that she cannot amend her story and change it at trial. This is similar to an actor memorizing a script. For actors, improvisation is fine—if you are in an improvisation troupe. There is nothing worse than looking at your partner on stage and realizing, as she looks at you wide-eyed, that she has obviously forgotten her next line, or perhaps all of her lines. You have to say asinine things like, "So, I bet you want to know if I sold the cherry orchard?" In a performance, the story and plot must be the same every show, every night. We expect the same from a witness.
3. A deposition allows you to see what kind of witnesses you may be dealing with at trial. This is where personality type comes in. Are they belligerent, rude, oblivious, nervous, unsure, stubborn, or just plain useless? A deposition is frequently used at trial to impugn or impeach a witness who testifies differently from their deposition testimony, so this is your chance to unravel an unsupported story from a witness you yourself are deposing.

A deposition will need to cover certain topics, just like an actor's appearance on a talk show will always end with the release dates of his upcoming movie or the name of his book, or when she will be on her book tour and where she will be next. This is not a coincidence; this is carefully planned. The deposition is your chance to have documents explained, to discover facts and admissions you want to reveal, and to be sure you have covered all the points in your outline. Careful preparation and crafting of your presentation of the questions is crucial for success.

What You Don't Know CAN Hurt You

A funny game a lot of talk shows play is a form of live, unrehearsed trivia, where a celebrity guest is asked random trivia questions to see how smart he or she is (no one really cares how smart Eva Longoria is, but it's still fun to watch). The audience takes joy in seeing the celebrity squirm and not know the answer, and they delight in thinking, "Ha! They're rich, but they had no idea that Maine is the toothpick capital of the world." This is a harmless funny game on television, but it is a powerful approach in the deposition. It is just as important to establish what the witness *doesn't know* as it is to find out what he does know. But how do we get this kind of admission from the person you are deposing? Let's look to the most famous TV hosts for their tips.

Hey, Come Here Often?

Don't think that when you flip on *The Oprah Winfrey Show* the show started right before Oprah walks onto the stage. Talk show hosts are no dummies; they pay actors/comedians/musicians/starving street performers to entertain the audience and get them warmed up before the show starts taping. The shows often shoot very early or very late at night, so the energy level must be manipulated and maintained. There is singing, games, partial nudity (well, maybe not on the *Oprah* set, but on Jimmy Fallon's set for sure), and other shenanigans. The point is, the audience is warmed up by the time the big show starts.

As a litigator, be sure to use small talk to loosen up the witness and define the relationship he or she has with you. It is a lot easier to talk when you know exactly how the relationship is defined. It doesn't have to be friendly, although this can often be a good technique. Intimidation also works. Letterman is notorious for badgering young performers who appear on his show, and ends up getting a great performance from them. When you say things like, "For the record," it may freeze up a witness. Maybe this is what you want. If you are looking for a more open approach, try, "So, did you say that you go dancing almost every night?" This approach feels less like an interrogation and more like a conversation.

Don't Interrupt!

One of the most simple and most powerful tricks TV hosts use is to simply let the guest talk. The guest is in the spotlight, and he or she will naturally feel the need to fill in gaps or silence, to be a fun, interesting, or helpful guest. It's the same with witnesses. Once they stop talking, just look at them, nod, and think in your mind, "Go on . . ." This will reflect on your face and body, subliminally urging them to keep talking. This usually works like a charm, because people love to talk about themselves and what they know. It's human nature. Even if they have been coached not to say certain things, you can use this technique to get the information out of them. Imagine a TV host asking a simple question of a guest regarding how hard she is working lately. This is the kind of question that just may lead to the discovery that Drew Barrymore sleeps naked with her favorite stuffed rabbit. She acts shocked that she admitted it, and the audience eats it up. When Drew is naked, everyone is happy, especially David Letterman.

Just like a guest on a talk show, the urge is there for a witness to volunteer information. Most of us have a desire to please that is hard to suppress. Witnesses almost feel like they are there to educate. Play on this urge. This is exactly the frame of mind you want the deposed to be in. They will feel a strong urge to add to their answer with additional facts or to explain something to help their cause. Try to connect and support that impulse they are having.

If you are finished with the question and the answer has been offered, just wait, and look at the witness expectantly. Ask if that is all she recollects, as this will urge her to continue to talk. When there is a silence—and this is very important—do not ask another question. Just give the "Tell me more" look, with a friendly and interested look on your face. Have you ever watched a talk show host do an interview and he barely has to say a word, because the star practically interviews herself? It's the exact same thing.

Keep It Open

In general, the more open-ended the question, the better. Start broad and then narrow down to specifics as the deposed offers more and more information. It is much easier to ask for clarification of a salient point after the deposed has raised it than to go directly after it in your initial question. If you seek admission of a particular fact, leading questions will almost always be more effective and appropriate than a direct attack. Start with the open-ended questions, then move toward the leading questions. Let's explore the difference.

Open-ended questions help establish rapport, gather information, and increase understanding between the parties. Open-ended questions help witnesses loosen up and tell their story in their own words.

Examples of open-ended questions:
1. Tell me about your relationship with your parents.
2. Would you tell me more about_____?
3. Could you help me understand_____?
4. What do you want to do next?
5. What are the good things about your job?
6. Can you tell me about your relationship with your boss?
7. How do you feel about that? (A classic therapist question to get people to open up.)

Leading questions are questions that suggest the answer or contain the information the examiner is looking for in the question, and can often be answered with yes or no. In a courtroom, leading questions are open to objection, because they compromise the witness and potentially taint the evidence that he or she provides. Still, if you are in search of admission or impeachment material in a deposition, leading questions are absolutely appropriate. And, as you all know, sometimes they are worth the risk even in the courtroom.

Examples of leading questions:

1. You were at McVibe's bar on the night of August 15th, weren't you?
2. You were driving to Florida on the night of December 31st, 1976, were you not?
3. You opened the box, correct?
4. You strapped the water skis to your feet, right?

Sometimes leading questions end the same way, with a tag, by saying, "Right?" "Is that correct," or "Weren't you?" Instead of using tags, experiment with using your tone of voice to imply that this is not a statement, but a question. Raising the pitch in your voice at the end will have the same effect.

Quick Tip 5.1: Depose Your Coffee Maker or a Potted Plant

At this point in the chapter, it is time to start working on what we have learned. I am now going to ask you to depose your dog (or potted plant, or coffee maker). You must pick an object so you can practice exploring your line of vision and when and how you make eye contact. Perhaps your coffee maker just decided to stop working one day, on a day that you really needed coffee. Maybe the dog decided to eat your garage door opener, and there is no spare. Practice the skills we have covered so far, such as loosening up the witness, not interrupting (use your imagination as to how they would respond), and alternating between open-ended and leading questions.

When You Have More Time!

There is nothing worse than watching a TV host interview a guest and it is going terribly (slow, boring, and low-energy). Maybe the actor is just tired, or maybe he is on peyote. Either way, the host's job is to somehow pull any bit of information from them to salvage the interview. For litigators, this is very similar to the last call for questions before you close all the doors on this deposition. Try saying things like, "You haven't left anything out, have you?" "Is there anything else you can think of that you want to share?" "Was anyone else there?" That way, you know you have absolutely opened and closed every door you can.

Dictate the Tempo of the Deposition

If you want to take control of the deposition, you have to take control of the pace. Do not give the witness time to pause and think before answering every question. At some point the witness will get tired or feel under pressure. This is where a sense of urgency in their answering is very powerful.

You can dictate the tempo of the deposition by:

1. how quickly you speak;
2. how tight or tense your body is;
3. how much movement you use as you talk;
4. constant eye movement; and
5. vocal tone.

Quick Tip 5.2: As Easy as Counting to 10

Practice counting out loud from 1 to 10, using different types of tempo, such as frantic, confused, contemplative, or enraged. Once you master the ability to be comfortable with dictating the tempo of simple numbers in sequence, it's a lot easier to then apply this tool to your questioning.

Call It Like You See It

It is important for talk show hosts to acknowledge what they see. If a guest comes out in a very low-cut dress, it's absolutely imperative that at some point the host acknowledges that he really has not heard a word she has said but that he really likes her dress. Or, if an actor is flying around, jumping on chairs, or running into the audience, the host must not pretend it's not happening or look away to be polite, or try to avoid discussion of the fact that he just peed in the potted fake plant on the set. Similarly, if you ask a fabulous question and the witness confers with his attorney before answering, call him on it! Say something like, "Now that you have had a chance to discuss the question with your attorney, . . ." This adds a level of intimidation for the witness. Their need for a safety blanket is now on public record. It may just convince them to not ask their attorney for advice on the next difficult question you pose.

Exercise 5.1: Secret Word

Secret Word is a really fun improvisation game that will help you fine-tune the skill of getting other people to say what you want them to say. This game must be played with at least one other person, but all you need are yourselves. No paper, pen, or props are required. I will explain the games as if three people are playing, and you can adapt as needed.

Player Three is sent out of the room, and while she is gone the remaining two players will think of a word that you don't say very often—for example, *corndog*.

When Player Three comes back into the room, the goal of the two players is to say one short sentence to get the third person to guess the answer. So, Player One might look at her and say, "You eat this at the fair." If Player Three guesses incorrectly and says "cotton candy," Player Two must offer a different hint, like "It has a stick in the middle." If Player Three says "Popsicle," she has had two incor-

> rect guesses in a row, which means she has to do something embarrassing, such as squawk like a chicken in the office in front of everyone. Now back to the secret word. If after two more rounds of guesses Player Three still has not guessed *corndog*, she is the big loser and can be harassed as much as you deem appropriate. Now switch: a new player goes outside. This game allows you to practice getting a witness to say what you want, and it is tons of fun.

Closing Argument

The more depositions you take, the better you will get. Be sure to remain professional while exploring all the tools you have to get what you want. Your goal is to glean as much information from the deposed as possible, and hopefully have them respond to you in the way that you desire. Who knows, you may have a career as a late-night talk show host as a retirement option! If that doesn't work out, the CIA is always in need of good interrogators (or so I hear).

Chapter 6

Improvisation

Opening Statement: Think Fast or Come In Last

Attorneys are often placed in situations where they need to speak without any prepared material. This happens at social gatherings, business luncheons, shareholder meetings, and even in court, unfortunately. The attorney who is prepared to utilize a sharp wit and quick thinking will master these situations. Improvisation will help you develop these skills so the next time you are asked to speak in public impromptu, you are ready for battle.

Improvisation games are a staple in acting schools for developing strong instincts, quick decision making, and the ability to work with others on the fly. Whether an attorney is in a client meeting, judge's chambers, or at the negotiating table, he or she must be able to recall information quickly, develop rapid-fire response skills, and work in tandem with co-counsel when necessary to develop a story or answer in the heat of the moment. Too often attorneys bog down when put on the spot because they have not had time to prepare a well-thought-out response. The techniques taught in this chapter will develop skills that will make you quicker on your feet and also prevent you from putting your foot in your mouth.

Improvisation allows an actor to create specific characters in particular situations. A skilled actor will rely on personal experience, training, and instincts to create an onstage presence that complements what is happening in real time. Every lawyer should have this type of intuition and flexibility when it comes to client communication, bonding with co workers, or even influencing the jury. Are you able to "go with the flow" and change your "character" to drive home the story you are trying to tell?

Sometimes the role of concerned citizen is the ideal character when representing a plaintiff who has been harmed by a large corporation. If you are representing the defendant corporation, your role may be that of a rational and stringent interpreter of the law. What if you are negotiating a multimillion-dollar land sale for your client, a stubborn old-timer, and the buyer is a scheming developer? What traits will each want to see in the attorney handling the matter? Perhaps each one will be looking for something different. Improvisation skills will help an attorney juggle situations like this.

Improvisation Skills

Before we can proceed to the fancy tricks that have allowed me to avoid a speeding ticket, we need to discuss the skills we are looking to acquire. As a modern attorney, it is vital that you are able to demonstrate all the skills the most polished improviser displays. Think of famous actors whose background is in improvisation. Many of the actors cast in *Saturday Night Live* came from an improvisation background. This program produced such comedy stars as Mike Myers, Chris Farley, John Belushi, and Tina Fey. Improvisation comedy techniques have also been used in television and stand-up comedy, in hit shows such as HBO's *Curb Your Enthusiasm*, and the ABC television series *Whose Line Is It Anyway.*

All of these actors have a few vital traits in common: They are able to think on their feet, develop ideas quickly, listen carefully, be in the moment, and are comfortable with their dependable and spontaneous strong choices. Who knows if any of them would make great lawyers, but there is no reason that you cannot pillage their techniques in order to make you a better attorney. A quick wit and sharp tongue are not only necessary traits professionally, but can save you a great deal of trouble and even some money when you negotiate your next vehicle purchase.

Many lawyers strive for an improvisational tone in the courtroom or while working with clients. Lawyers should work to make their written words sounds as if they are being pulled from inside, as if they are finding the words and using them as they occur in the moment. But how do you do this? I'm going to teach you.

The reason improvisation is a good starting point for these skills is that it really is a chance to *play.* Using Improvisation exercises allows you to explore all kinds of characters by using feelings, physical behaviors, and mannerisms to get what you want. Improv allows us to concentrate on what is happening, not what is going to happen. Pretty deep, huh? Okay, let's play!

Warming Up

When I was studying improvisation at Second City in Chicago, it was fascinating to see how different instructors have such different opinions on warming up. Some instructors rolled their eyes at us if they saw us in the corner before class, stretching or doing vocal warm-ups. They would just bark, "Get on stage! What are we, in 'The Nutcracker'?" Other instructors would spend more than half the class talking us through lots of physical, vocal, and emotional warm-ups to help relax us, open us up, and allow natural and unforced performances.

Now, the stakes are lower for actors than they are for lawyers. If I do a bad improv show, my ego may be bruised, but a few beers at the local pub will most likely make me feel better. If a lawyer does a poor job improvising, however, this can cost you money, success, and maybe even your license. It's hard to buy beer without money and a job.

For me, a physical warm-up is vital, yet so many lawyers will just step into a room full of people with no warm-up at all, except for a coffee they chugged down as they gathered their material and notes. Think about it like this. Let's say we were all on a volleyball team, but we only got together for the actual games. We never practiced. Now, imagine that our opposing team practiced three times a week, and when they hit the sand they were a finely oiled machine. Would we enjoy this experience? Hell no! Because we would suck! We would be falling all over the place, out of breath and begging for the game to end.

Public speaking is the same. We seem to expect to just "be good" without any kind of warm-up, rehearsal, or emotional and physical preparation. Every day, lawyers Improvise—with their clients, over the phone, and to the judge. We have to train ourselves to be the best possible version of ourselves when we are speaking on the fly. This next section will list ways to get there that do not include a double shot of espresso at your desk.

All of these exercises are things that you can do at home before you leave the house, or even in the bathroom at work, and they will greatly enhance your ability to relax and be flexible. At every audition I go to, I arrive 20 minutes early to warm up in the car. Every once in a while I will walk in assuming I have 20 minutes to warm up and relax away my jitters, and someone will say, "Laura! Great! We are actually running ahead, so just come on back!"

How to Be Loose and Ready to Go

> ### Exercise 6.1: Three-Minute Rag Doll
>
> Rag doll position is a simple and easy way to focus your mind and relax your body. It involves the body slowly collapsing from a standing position, like wallpaper peeling off a wall. Stand with your feet shoulder-width apart, knees slightly bent. Your head leads, using its weight to naturally and slowly lower your body toward the floor, vertebra by vertebra. Eventually your knees will still be bent and your arms hanging down almost touching the floor, and you will be using only the minimum number of muscles to keep yourself from falling over. If you feel tension in a certain area, just continue to breathe deeply, and shake your head or arms out to remind your body to let go. As you peel up slowly, your head is the last thing to get into alignment. This feels great and prepares your mind and body for performance.

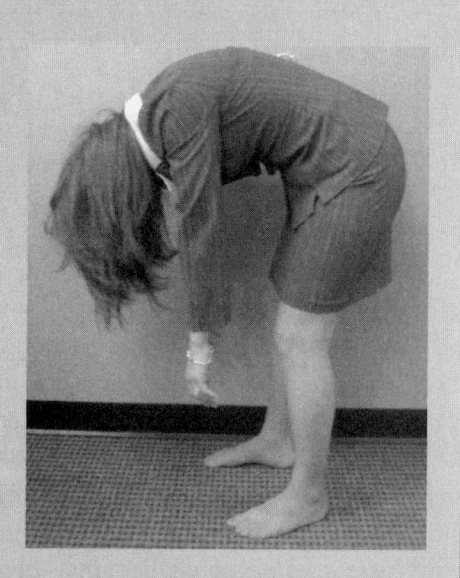

How to Improvise When Put on the Spot

A simple improvisation game called ABC is fun to play with friends but can easily be played on your own. This exercise works toward building your confidence in what comes out of your mouth and shutting down the inner critic that distracts you from your fabulous first instincts.

> **Exercise 6.2: ABC Improvisation**
>
> In ABC Improvisation, first pick a topic, like "The craziest weather I have ever seen." Now, you will tell a story that has to follow the letters of the alphabet, so the first sentence will start with A, next sentence with B, and so on. For example, I might say, "**A** really cool thunderstorm happened when I was in Ohio. **B**ecause it was nighttime, we got a little scared. **C**olored streaks of lightning were coming right at us. **D**on't think I wasn't scared out of my mind!"

Do not overanalyze your story. I realize that this is extremely difficult for most attorneys. It may not really make sense or flow the way you want it to. The most important thing is to practice just shortening the gap between thought and words, and staying calm.

This game is also a great way to practice not using fillers, such as "like," "um," "ah," "so," and "but–um." Play this game while you are cooking dinner to get your brain into improvisation mode and think on the fly while engaged in an activity. Change the topic every time so you are challenging yourself. Make sure to go all the way through the alphabet until you hit Z.

Your Body Will Improvise, Whether You Want It To or Not!

A wonderful improvisation exercise to get you connected to your body is called a "space walk." It takes me awhile to convince a lawyer to really get into a space walk, so do this exercise when (a) you have a private space, and (b) no one is watching. This exercise will challenge you to let go of inhibitions, which is a crucial step in learning to speak quickly and accurately.

When an actor does a space walk, it is a way to explore certain types of characters and how to demonstrate different qualities physically. For example, if I was preparing my character for a movie, I might simply walk through the space, exploring how my character walks, how she moves her body, where she puts her weight, whether she is loose and flowing or tight and tense, whether she leads with her nose or chest as she walks, and simply finding her sense of energy. Why is this important for a lawyer? How do you want to be seen as you move through different environments?

Body language will always tell your story whether you want to or not. Imagine my surprise when, on a recent trip to my neighborhood bakery, the owner looked at me and said, "Tough day? You look like you need a cookie." It was funny and we both laughed, but it was amazing that he could tell my real mood based on my body language, and saw right through my fake smile as I walked in the door. We have to understand and be able to control our body language. Our posture tells a story, and we can use our body to tell a story that will persuade our listeners to see things our way. For more information on this topic, see Chapter 4, Being In Your Body.

Exercise 6.3: Space Walk

To start, simply walk around your room or office as you normally do, taking note of your posture, your speed, and the tension in your body. Now imagine you are a very high-strung, excited person. How would this person walk? Does the pose change? How about where he might hold his tension? Now walk like a person who is confused. Does your eye line change? Does your posture change?

Now we can add your voice to your walk. What types of thing might a person say who is rich? Poor? Paranoid? Lonely? Hyper? Devastated? Ecstatic? Once you get over your initial apprehension of randomly talking out loud while moving through space, you can see how much power your body has in telling a story. A jury will make an immediate assumption about you based on how you move through space. What kind of story do you want to tell? What kind of emotion do you want to share? Your body will tell your story a lot more honestly than your words, so it is vital that we learn how to change and be flexible based on the information we want to share with our audience.

Explore and Heighten

A very important concept in improvisation is "explore and heighten." When actors are in a scene, we want to explore and heighten what happens. The scene changes, it transforms, and it becomes bigger somehow. This concept can be used by attorneys in client meetings, depositions, and at the negotiating table to great effect.

In real life, humans tend to do the opposite. If a friend says, "Man, I've been feeling really run down lately, I hope I'm not getting sick," we will say things like "Oh, I bet you just need a good night's sleep." But if we were to explore and heighten, you might say "Yes, I noticed you've been looking terrible lately. It's probably swine flu. Seems like everyone in the office is getting it. I hope it isn't fatal. Most people end up dying from swine flu, especially people *your* age."

Now, this may be fun to say to the annoying co-worker who eats tuna every day at his desk, but you probably don't want to use this technique to insult opposing counsel. (Or maybe you do!) This is just an example of how much fun it can be to explore and heighten. Rather than purposely dampening our conversations or presentations with language that drives the concepts down and minimizes them, we can heighten the language to dive into new areas and really drive a point home.

In the courtroom or when speaking in front of others, if you are brave enough to explore and heighten, your words will fly through the room and have immediate impact. Here is an exercise to practice the concept of explore and heighten.

> **Exercise 6.4: Explore and Heighten**
>
> 1. Choose a physical activity (e.g., throwing a baseball into the air).
> 2. Play with how you throw it; it is not a fancy scene, just an action.
> 3. Allow the baseball to change and become something new—a baby, a snake, a winning lottery ticket.
> 4. Explore and heighten the new activity, and experience the moment of transformation from one object to the next.

> Experiencing the moment of transformation is huge in improvisation. As listeners, we want to be entertained. We all want to be kept captivated. Are you brave enough to take the time to truly experience a moment of transformation when speaking with others? Heightening is simply making what you have to say important. If you do not show or tell me what is important, I might miss it. Get it?

Next up is a really fun game. Again, all the games listed in this book can be played with any number of people. If you have fun-loving friends, try a few of these games at the local bar after work. If that seems weird to you, you can also play on your own. In the last exercise, we practiced using *actions* to explore and heighten a situation. Now we will use *words* to practice exploring and heightening.

> **Exercise 6.5: Comma**
>
> In this game, two people are having dinner (or just you if all of your friends are lame). As you are acting out having dinner as different characters (maybe a football coach and one of his players), your partner will say "Comma" during one of your lines. This means the actors are paused, and the actor that was interrupted must stand aside and give us a 30-second monologue, or soliloquy if you will, exploring the thought they were just interrupted from. Do not use law stuff as material when you are your making up characters. Argue and pontificate over such things as "What is better, smooth or crunchy peanut butter?" After 30 seconds have passed, simply go back to the conversation you were having as if nothing has happened.

Every word has the potential to drive the scene. Heightening is not screaming. Heightening develops the relationship you have with your listener and allows him to get inside your head. If you're not fully exploring your thoughts for your audience, how will they know what you are trying to say? If you are playing this game by yourself, simply set a stopwatch to go off every 40 seconds or so, interrupting you from your conversation, or just interrupt yourself randomly. This game is tons of fun and really allows you to develop the skills you need to build spontaneous excitement in your speech.

During an improv scene, you should be able to show immediate emotional changes. This is something lawyers often struggle with. They know how they want to feel, or should feel, but actually showing it can be difficult. An emotional change is again simply a transformation, and transformational moments are the "Aha!" moments you are looking for when trying to convince someone that your argument is correct.

> **Exercise 6.6: What Is in Your Pocket?**
>
> This is a very cool exercise you can do every day to show transformation in your speech. Before you start your speech, know what is in your pocket. For example, before I go to a networking event, I might imagine that in my pocket is a $1,000 bill, and I plan on giving it to the person who is the most interesting to talk to. Now all my conversations are intense, almost game show–like, filled with excitement. Is this my winner? Or, perhaps if you are arguing a case where you need to be very persuasive, you could imagine you have a letter from the judge that says he is going to rule in your favor. Now you are relaxed and confident as you speak, because you know that all you have to do is put the icing on the cake.

This trick also works well for nerves. If I am very nervous going into an audition, I will imagine I have a first-class plane ticket to Hawaii in my pocket, which is where I am heading right after the audition. Just the thought of lying on the beach, getting a Mai Tai from the swim-up bar, and hitting happy hour in a tiki hut is enough to make me less nervous and just a happier person in general. I am also less attached to what they are thinking of me and my performance. It really works!

Eye Contact and Grounding

Another thing improvisers are taught to do is to make eye contact with our scene partners and ground ourselves before the scene starts. This is vital for litigators, because you need that moment to center yourself, with breath and physical calm, before you launch into your speech. It sets the tone for your entire presentation. Remember, first impressions last the longest. If you are grounded and prepared, it is much easier to look that witness right in the eye and deliver a cross that leaves them crying and admitting everything. Use of eye contact can be difficult to master, but deadly once you have the hang of it.

Diction

In an improvised presentation, the first thing that usually falls apart is diction. If we are not totally confident in what we are about to say, we tend to muffle our words in order to hide any half-truths or incorrect statements we might accidentally let slip out of our mouths. There is not an attorney or a toddler alive who hasn't used this technique to try to weasel out of a jam. If you practice the exercise below every day, I promise you will have much more power in your speech, so that when you do have to improvise, we can hear everything you are saying. If we can hear you and you speak confidently, we assume you know what you are talking about. There is no need to mumble. It is that simple.

> **Exercise 6.7: Rhyme Time**
>
> Memorize this rhyme:
>
> > Whether the weather be cold
> > Whether the weather be hot
> > We'll be together, whatever the weather
> > Whether we like it or not.
>
> Once you have it memorized, try it in lots of ways (good activity for the shower or bath). Say the rhyme soft but intense, fast, no tone at all, full-tilt, as Kermit the Frog, as a stoner surfer dude, as Al Pacino in a big dramatic court scene, as a matter-of-fact businessman, as an amused Donald Trump, etc.
>
> This also works as a great vocal warm-up, so you are vocally relaxed. This exercise helps the words flow out of you and keeps your mouth, jaw, and lips relaxed. Plus it is just fun to say.

How to Be Better at Improvisation

Life happens so quickly that we often experience major life events and never take the time to really absorb what happened. This is especially true for lawyers. You deal with such high-paced, intense, often detailed encounters that if you do not take the time to take a step back, you will never grow and develop your speaking skills. As an actor, I have always kept a professional journal that I use for personal development in my field. Anytime I have an audition, I will list what I wore, whom the audition was for, names of people I met, how I felt it went, how I could improve next time, and a copy of any documents I received. I will also set a goal for myself and note whether I achieved it. For example, "I will maintain perfect posture," or "I will address everyone by their names when I leave."

This is an incredible tool for lawyers to use as well. Notes should be taken after networking events, speaking engagements, important meetings, or any interactions where you would like to improve your presence and speaking abilities. The only way to figure out why you were drenched in sweat at the last meeting with your boss is to break down what you did and how you did it. This may be the tool that helps you realize that wool suits are a terrible idea for a big presentation, or that you felt underprepared and thus spoke far too quickly, or that you were so busy pushing your opinion that you forgot to really listen to the feedback and questions that were directed to you.

After any public speaking event, whether it's a social gathering or a big presentation, ask yourself:

1. What did I experience?
2. What did I feel?
3. Was I able to live in the moment and be in the response mode (instead of just waiting for your turn to talk)?
4. What worked?
5. What did I notice?
6. What changed?
7. Did I create a relationship?
8. Did I both give and take focus?

If you spend 10 minutes answering these questions every time you speak, your skills will become razor-sharp and you will never slip into bad habits or patterns that sabotage your professional development and achievements.

Closing Argument

Thinking on your feet and accessing your thoughts quickly and efficiently are crucial to success in the legal profession. As a practicing attorney, you may already have a natural ability in these areas. By training and developing these skills, you can walk into any environment confident that no situation will catch you entirely off-guard. And if it does, you'll be prepared to respond in an intelligent and professional manner.

We have all had those moments when we get home and only then think of the perfect witty comeback or jaw-dropping insight. Wouldn't it be great if we could access those thoughts at the moment when we really need them? Improvisation is the secret. Practice is the key.

Chapter 7

Storytelling

Opening Statement: Telling Stories Ain't the Same as Lying

Storytelling is a tradition that has been around as long as humans have had the inclination to become bored and desire entertainment. We used to sit around fires and in caves entertaining one another with stories of the hunt, or the gods, and of course stories about the idiot in the cave next door and his penchant for picking berries with someone other than his cave mate. Those with the most talent for storytelling became leaders and influential members in their communities. Shamans, bards, royal advisors, and tribal elders became institutions in many cultures. Communities turned to them for guidance, entertainment, and information. Attorneys are a natural extension of these historical storytellers.

While at trial, an attorney's responsibility is to present his or her client's story in a manner that will persuade the judge or jury to see the case through the lens of the client. A good attorney already knows how to draft an argument in a way that places the client in his best light, but now he must present this story to the court. Actors utilize techniques to shape scenes and entire scripts so that the message is conveyed as a whole, rather than a mishmash of unconnected parts. It is easy to practice one line, or to make sure you nail a couple of major points, but a good trial attorney will shape his entire case as one large story to best present his client's argument. This chapter will teach attorneys a five-point structure for storytelling that will apply directly to the entire presentation of a case.

The Challenges of Telling a Good Story

In terms of storytelling, actors and litigators face similar challenges. We have to stand up in front of strangers, colleagues, and friends and tell a story in such a credible way that the audience leaves completely convinced of our tale, our message, and our character's journey. Attorneys get three years of training in the law, covering numerous subjects, but strangely there are no acting classes in law school. Trial advocacy classes tend to focus on procedure, although they at least get you up in front of people and speaking. There is just no curriculum in place for developing the storytelling skills necessary to be a great litigator. Instead, you wait until your first case, which may be a simple DUI or an extremely complicated tort case, each equally terrifying and nerve-racking for a first-timer, and are expected to do your best with no public speaking training. I think that lawyers should have mandatory acting classes, and actors should have mandatory classes on how to get out of a public nudity charge. But that is another story, and a good one at that!

Not Just Another "Case"

When people approach a lawyer in a desperate attempt for help, they tend to get a bit miffed when their problem is referred to as a "case" or a "matter." To them, this is no case, to be opened and closed at will. This is their life, this is their story. As long as litigators remain cold and detached and call the story a case, an incident, etc., they can never really slip into the passion required to be a fabulous storyteller. We all have our stories to tell, don't we? There is something unique about everyone! Where you grew up, how you grew up, your family's values, where you went to school and how you got there, how you met your current husband/wife/chiropractor/spiritual adviser/ bookie/ therapist. These are all important stories to the individual. What kinds of pets you have, and why, are a part of your story. Whether you are superstitious, obsessive-compulsive, or are more relaxed than a stoned frat boy playing frisbee golf—these are all stories, and all of them will play into how you represent your client.

I understand that attorneys must be detached from their cases to a certain degree. Don't forget, I'm married to an attorney. I can tell when a case is weighing on my husband too heavily. I'm not saying that you need to take others' problems on as your own. Truly feeling each loss and wholly sharing in every defeat will beat a lawyer down quickly. However, a certain amount of empathy is required for an attorney to present his client's argument in a way that will sell the jury or judge.

Actors love being the center of attention. That's why we are constantly telling stories. Often, to make a story better, we will take a situation that happened in our lives and exaggerate it for dramatic purposes. This embellishment is not only considered appropriate but is expected. The competition for an engaging story that wins over the room is tough with actors, and even tougher with stand-up comedians. When I was a young girl, the tiles in our bathroom right under the shower head had caved in, and my father had removed them in order for them to be replaced. (This ended up taking over two weeks, to everyone's dismay. Sponge baths for everyone.) One day I had a friend over, and as we were washing our hands in the bathroom, she said, "What happened to your wall?" I replied, "Oh, well, it's a pretty bad thing. My mom was showering one day, and suddenly a hand came SMASHING thru the wall, and this bad guy was hiding in the wall. He tried to strangle my mom as she was showering, but she screamed and scared him off. So now my dad is going to put a cement wall back there so no more bad guys can sneak into the house like that."

Pretty good, huh? Little Cindy's eyes grew wide in horror, tears welling up. "Well," I said cheerfully, "let's go play with my Barbie dolls!"

Why did I do this? Even at age 7, I was such a storytelling junkie that I could not resist. This little lie was not preplanned; I just came up with it on the spot. Although this may be more of a sign that I needed full-time counseling, I prefer to say that storytelling is fun and is meant to affect the listener. Who is the listener for litigators? The judge? Sometimes. However, if there is a jury, they are your listening audience. We want the jury to hang on our every word, seeing the image of the scary bad guy's hand bust through the tile, grab my poor mother's wet, skinny little neck, and hear her shrill screams echoing through the house as the bad guy panicked and scurried back inside the wall.

Obviously, you can't outright lie to a jury. Nonetheless, you can learn how to take the facts of a case and present them to the jury in a way that will have them captivated with you, your client, and your version of events. Are you ready to tell a story that will captivate and sway a jury? Well, let's get started.

If you are a little rusty in the storytelling department, it is important to understand that there is a standard structure you must follow to tell a story that the audience can follow, relate to, and comprehend.

Quick Tip 7.1: Kid Lit

A great way to explore the keys to a great story is to stop by your local bookstore on the way home from work and wander around the children's book section. You will be reminded of all the wonderful techniques used in storytelling, with colorful pictures, tactile pages, scratch-and-sniff pages, fun and descriptive rhyming, and larger-than-life characters or plot lines. Use these books as inspiration for your hero's story when you are in the brainstorming phase of a case.

Stanislavski the Storyteller

I am going to introduce you to the actor's source for becoming a storyteller. Constantin Stanislavski was a Russian actor and director at the Moscow Art Theatre. His approach to acting was the result of many years spent studying how someone can control through performance the most intangible and uncontrollable aspects of human behavior, such as emotions and inspiration. The most influential acting teachers, including Michael Chekhov, Lee Strasberg, Stella Adler, Sanford Meisner, Uta Hagen, and Ivana Chubbuck, all refer to Stanislavski in their work.

One of Stanislavski's methods for achieving the truthful pursuit of a character's objective was his "magic if." Actors were required to ask many questions of their characters and themselves. This is typically called a character analysis. One of the first questions an actor has to ask is, "What if I were in the same situation as my character?" The "magic if" allowed actors to transcend the confines of reality or their minimal past experiences by asking what would occur "if" circumstances were different, or "if" the circumstances were to happen to them.

The "magic if" makes a huge difference in a litigator's passion and attachment to a case. Most litigators I work with can barely scrounge up the tiniest bit of authentic passion and attachment to the story. More often than not, they approach a case in a mechanical and matter-of-fact way, as if the case is merely a message they have been sent to relay, much like, "Hey, your mom called earlier." Did you relay the message? Sure. Do we care? Nope. So how can you make us care? It is not about putting on a ridiculous swagger and rolling around the courtroom all bluff and clownlike. It is more about being brave enough to be real. To be real, you have to strip yourself naked for all to see the real you. You want to tell a story than *means* something to you.

> **Exercise 7.1:**
> **Putting the "What If" Exercise to Work for You**
>
> This exercise will help you think like a storyteller instead of like a lawyer. It is truly a skill, finding language that both sings and communicates precisely. In this exercise we will use *"What If?"* to create a one-minute story on any topic you like. Some suggestions might be your first job, the first car you drove, or the day you decided to become a lawyer. Set a timer to go off after one minute to keep you on track. This exercise forces you to get to the meat of the story quickly and create an arc in a very short amount of time. Next, set the timer for 30 seconds, then 10 seconds. It may be that the 30-second version had more energy and flow than the 60-second story, because you were motivated to share the information in the clearest way possible. Use this approach as you prepare your story for a jury to practice being naked and true—no fillers or fluff allowed.

Being Naked, Being Truthful

While we are talking about being naked, here's a great story. When I was studying theatre and drama at the University of Toronto, our first-year class had a day that changed us forever. We were only a few months into school, still full of nerves and ego and the ability to somehow party all night, get two hours of sleep, and be in class by 8 a.m. the next day. (This skill is now long gone.)

Our instructor looked at us very seriously one morning and said he had an assignment for the next week's class that was worth 40 percent of our final grade. Our ears perked up. He said that to truly be a successful actor you must be willing to be naked on stage, both physically and emotionally. You had to strip away fears, self-consciousness, and self-awareness. You had to let the audience look at you, really look at you, and be able to stand there completely at ease with nothing to hide.

He stated that the next week we would all do a strip show down to as little clothing as we felt comfortable in, but complete nudity was preferred. We could bring costumes, music, or anything we wanted to make the exercise our own. This was not a joke, he stated. Anyone who does not participate is obviously too fearful to be an actor and will fail the assignment.

When he left the room we all looked at each other with shock, giggles, and complete fear. For the next six days a small group of girls in the class, myself included, got together, decided on our outfits, the music we would strip to, and the elaborate routine. We drank a bottle of wine to relax, and then practiced in front of each other. We would hoot and holler, cheering each other on. None of us ever got completely naked as we practiced, but we all swore we would on the big day.

A few people stated they absolutely refused to do the exercise. It was inappropriate and degrading and stupid, and they planned to approach the administration to voice their concerns. A few people decided to use the humorous approach, undressing to reveal funny outfits like foil underwear, neon pubic hair, or balled up socks to enhance their features.

To be sure this was a real assignment; we even approached the older classes in the program, the second-, third-, and fourth-year students. They bemoaned that same exercise and how terrible it was, and told us that everyone who took this particular instructor's class had to do it. It was just the professor's approach. They laughed at our fear and told us that they all got through it, so we would too.

The day of the exercise, I think we were the most well groomed we had ever been. Everyone smelled clean and fresh like shaving cream and perfume and adrenalin. The teacher said we would be performing in alphabetical order, by last name. My last name at the time was Mulhall, so I breathed a sigh of relief that I had time to gauge how naked people were really going to get. As the first actor stood up and stood center stage, we were all suddenly very uncomfortable. Was I ready to see all my closest colleagues, friends, and competition naked? I told myself I *had* to do it, but actually doing it would be a different matter. To make it worse, it was just in a regular classroom, with scratchy old carpet and fluorescent lights.

Just as the first actor was about to start, our teacher said, "Now before we start I need to tell you, this is all just a joke! Ha-ha!" We all exploded in relief and agitation and embarrassment. This fake nudity assignment was apparently a tradition that goes on every year, and all the older students play along to help seal the deal. A few members of the class were actually disappointed, as we had put so much thought and planning into our performance!

What is the point of this story? That theatre school is way more fun than law school? That's true, but that's not my actual point. It was indeed a good lesson in how far we were willing to go to expose ourselves in front of others, not only physically but emotionally. It takes bravery to offer your true self, to stand on the stage alone, to tell your story. Being truthful is something you have to acquire through honest contemplation of the person you really are.

Quick Tip 7.2: Being Truthful for a Day

For one day, try only telling the truth. This is a very hard exercise. When we alert our mother-in-law that we don't actually like the holiday gift she gave us (a one-year subscription to *Kitten World*), or tell our neighbors that we don't want to go to their damn party (where you know they will try to sell you a week of their timeshare in Nogales, Mexico), or tell the masseuse that we did not enjoy our massage (she smelled like cigarettes and lunchmeat), we risk offending or upsetting our listener. But it can still be fun to try out for a day.

Start with the casual questions people will ask you. "How's your day going so far?" Instead of telling the coffee barista, "Fine, thanks," just tell her the truth. "Oh, it's been pretty disastrous so far! I woke up late, spilled milk on my pants, and I have to work late tonight!" An amazingly honest and real interaction will occur, and you may end up having the most fun and connected conversation with the barista you have ever had, despite the fact that you have been stopping at the same coffee shop for six months.

Being truthful opens you up to real conversations, connecting to real human beings, and offers you the inspiration for all storytelling. Just be selective when you choose to be truthful. Not everyone is equipped emotionally to handle such honest responses. Use your best judgment; you are an attorney, after all.

Connecting to the Audience

For litigators, the audience is often the jury. Your story has to offer them an understandable, clear plot that they can relate to. All great movies and stories contain universal truths that allow us to connect to the story and characters. To say, "Yes! I have felt that way!" "Yes, I know how hard that struggle is!" "Yes, if that was me, I would have felt the same way." Lawyers have the opportunity to tell the most wonderful, most tragic, and most elaborate stories. Lawyers tell stories of good versus evil, stories of right versus wrong, and stories of stagnation versus growth.

Adapting to Our Audience

The audience has a very important role in storytelling, for their minds are the canvas on which the speaker paints his tale. Oral storytelling involves much interaction between speaker and listener. This can be a challenge for the litigator. It is easier to stand up, do your thing, keep outside distractions to a minimum, and get out. Unfortunately, jurors' attention spans are shorter and more demanding these days. Jurors are more sophisticated, having access to so much information. Yet they are often less able to independently imagine or visualize a case. We live in a society where people are spoon-fed opinions. Guess who is holding the spoon in the courtroom? It better be you. If it's not, it will be opposing counsel.

Juries seem to need more visual stimulation; hence the influx of PowerPoint and other visual doodads that most speakers utilize. I personally refuse to use such things. I prefer me and a roomful of people. This helps me control where the attention goes. It drives me crazy when no one makes eye contact with me when I am speaking. I do appreciate that visual aids have great value, but there is a delicate balance in order to keep the story at the center of the action. There is nothing more interesting than an engaging speaker. People will hang on your words, and you won't need the crutch of visual aids. Here are some tips to engage the audience and involve them in the story.

1. **Get as close to the jury as you can.** Make eye contact. Move into the jury's space.

2. **Keep it simple**. Pare down to the heart of the story as soon as you can. Skip the fancy law talk and get to the universal truths fast.
3. **Stimulate their senses** so they feel, smell, touch, listen, and see vivid pictures.
4. **Describe the characters and environment,** and help the jury sympathize with the client's feelings.
5. **Don't be distracted by the feedback you receive from the jury.** If someone is shaking their head at you, you might interpret that as them thinking you are full of baloney, but really they are shaking their head as if to say, "I can't believe we are still talking about this, this lawyer is obviously on the side we all agree with!"

Deciding on Your Characters

The neat thing about storytelling is that you get to think about what character your client is represented by in the story. This involves imagination, creativity, and a splash of fun. Here are some examples of classic archetypes.

The Hero's Journey: Your Main Focus

Most often your client is the hero of the story. Yes, this is true even when he has been charged with a criminal offense. You saw *The Shawshank Redemption*, right? It is easy to mistakenly see your client as the victim, but that is not the stronger choice when it comes to storytelling. Actors always ask themselves, is this the strongest choice I can make? Do we like the concept of Luke Skywalker being a hero or a victim? He is a hero because he is called to action, into a strange and unfamiliar world. Or we can see him as a victim, dragged from his comfortable life and family. The word "victim" leaves a foul taste in our mouth. Save the "victim" roles for the characters in your story that are the true bad guys, the root of all the trouble, the instigators, and the first link to fail in the chain of negative events. Always make your client the hero.

You may realize there are many types of heroes, and you must choose carefully what type of hero your client is:

1. Warrior (Luke Skywalker, *Rocky*, *Braveheart*)
2. Creator (Frida Kahlo, Charlie Parker)
3. Caregiver (Jesus Christ, Buddha)
4. Outlaw (*Robin Hood, Thelma and Louise*)
5. Sage/Scholar (*Good Will Hunting, A Beautiful Mind,* Yoda)
6. Lover (*Shakespeare in Love, Moulin Rouge*)
7. Jester/Fool (Bill Murray, Will Farrell)
8. Innocent (Dorothy, Frodo)

It is important to also include your hero's *back story* as part of the current story (without diving too deep into it lest the judge interrupt you for relevance issues). This helps set up his past life as we knew it before this new struggle began. How can we know why someone does something without knowing where he comes from? The essence of the hero is not bravery or nobility, but self-sacrifice. We need to know what his life looked like before this chapter of the story began. We would never care about Cinderella if we didn't see the scenes where she is scrubbing floors or being mistreated by her stepsisters. The hero often pays a price to obtain his goal. Most important (listen up, this is the key), there is no heroism in battling a person. There is heroism in battling what a person represents. This is where the jury will feel good about making a decision in favor of the hero.

From here we can assign roles or archetypes to our other characters, like:

1. **The Mentor.** A character that aids or leads the hero. Think of the wise old man or woman, or a parent or teacher.
2. **The Blocker.** The guardian of the level your hero wants to be in; this is where the obstacle comes in on his journey.
3. **The Shape Shifter.** The shape shifter changes roles or personality in a confusing way. Perhaps their alliances and loyalty are uncertain, and the sincerity of their actions is often questionable. The hero can never be at peace around this character.
4. **The Shadow.** The shadow character represents things we don't like and would like to eliminate about both ourselves and others.
5. **The Villain.** There are many types of villains. We all know villains who act as the Traitor, the Evil Genius, the Lunatic,

the Backstabber, and the Schemer. (Sounds like Thanksgiving weekend at the in-laws.)

Choose Your Own Adventure

When I was a kid, I used to love reading "Choose Your Own Adventure" books. Throughout the story, there would be an option of two ways the story could go. As the reader, you were able to decide and turn to the page that connected your story until the next fork in the road. Eventually I would have read all the adventures and never failed to see the fun in rereading the ending I found most fulfilling or adventurous.

A court case is very similar, because the jurors get to choose their own adventure by deciding the end of the story. But, as an attorney and storyteller, you have a surprising amount of influence on what page they will turn to and how the story will end. What an incredible amount of power that jury has, and how lucky you are to be in a position to influence that power. The jurors must be reminded that they hold this power. Remind them they have the power to help the hero (your client). The choice of what page to turn to should be all but decided for them if you have done a good job at telling the story. Remember our archetypes from earlier? You are the mentor. The hero's transformation to the next chapter will occur once the jury has had its final say. It is up to the jury to transition our hero to a happy and just ending. The jury has to make the right choice, which is of course the choice that favors your client.

Exercise 7.2: One-Word Story

Here is a great exercise to play with friends. In One-Word Story, the goal is to create a story one word at a time. It is easy to preplan what to say in a story, but when we are forced to listen and respond to our group's words, the story changes and is redirected based on the previous word or direction in which the story seems to be heading. This game can be played with up to six people. Decide on a theme for the story, like "The day my dentist disappeared."

> As you go around in a circle, each person says one word, and together you will make a sentence. So it may sound like "one" "day" "my" "dentist" "went" "missing" "but" "I" "did" "not" "know" "why." There will be laughter as the story jumps or sentences run on. The point is to keep listening and make a story that makes sense, follows some kind of plot, and comes to a logical conclusion. It's a lot of fun and great to play at family events to get everyone involved. It also helps you develop the skill of changing a story on the fly as necessity dictates.

The Five-Point Structure for Storytelling

This is a basic five-point structure for storytelling that will help you shape your story into a tale that is recognizable to an audience and therefore easy to follow, understand, and relate to.

1. **Initial Harmony.** (Cinderella scrubs floors and has a crappy life.) The hero's back story.
2. **Beginning.** (The ball preparation and fairy godmother appears.)
3. **Body.** (Cinderella goes to ball, meets Prince Charming.)
4. **Climax.** (Cinderella feels like a fake.) Often the climax will showcase common themes such as demonstrating skill, integrity, moral struggle, or enduring hardships.
5. **Resolution.** (The shoe fits, he loves her, and she turns into a hottie.) Harmony is reestablished. Eventually, if the jury makes the right choice, the problem is solved and the story comes full circle to a restored or new harmony.

Preparation

Once you settle on a story and archetypes, you will want to spend plenty of time really exploring how it all fits together. It will take a considerable period of time and a number of retellings before a new story becomes your own. Therefore, you must practice your story every day.

1. **Review the story several times.** Your concentration will be tested by nerves when you are at trial.
2. **Analyze your choices.** Explore the pictures you want your listeners to see, and the mood you wish to create for the jury.
3. **Live with your story.** Stick with the story until the characters and plot become as real to you as people and places you know. You didn't experience what your client went through firsthand, so you have to use your imagination to place yourself in his shoes. Use the magic "what if" to help you care about the outcome as the story unfolds.
4. **Visualize it as you speak the words.** Imagine sounds, tastes, scents, and textures your hero experienced. Only when you see the story vividly yourself can you make your audience see it.

Exercise 7.1: Make Up a Story

This exercise is an opportunity to have a little fun and test your creativity. Using the archetypes listed above, create a handful of characters to inhabit your story. They can be anyone: mythical, real, or imagined. Now come up with a story for these characters using the Five-Point Structure to Storytelling. Let your imagination go wild! Tell the story to a friend, your spouse, or your kids, or write it down. If you write it down, practice telling the story out loud, even if you just tell it to your computer screen. Don't overthink this; it doesn't have to be perfect.

Now that you have invented your own story, it's time to shake it up. Take the characters from the story, but rearrange them to play the role of different archetypes. Now tell the story from the perspective of an entirely different hero. Imagine how different the story of Cinderella would be if the hero was the wicked stepmother!

Closing Argument

When it comes to storytelling, the more you practice, the more skilled you will become. Don't be afraid to try different methods of storytelling. Be creative. Expect to flop or end up playing much more low-key than you wanted to. The best of us will play it safe when we could have made a stronger choice. Don't be overly self-conscious—it's a story! Have fun! Share the passion of the hero's story. Not only will this aid you in presenting your client's case at trial, but it will make you infinitely more interesting at office holiday parties.

Chapter 8

Now You're the Acting Coach: How to Prepare Your Witness

Opening Statement: If You Train Them, You Will Win

Public speaking is the number-one fear in the world. If attorneys still get nervous when they step into the courtroom, imagine how their clients must feel. In this chapter, attorneys will learn techniques they can share with their witnesses to stave off stage fright and provide the best performance possible when testifying at a trial.

Preparing your own witness is similar to preparing an actor for an audition. Both have prepared lines and must be calm enough to remember and deliver them in a believable and honest manner. This chapter will also include techniques for rehearsing with clients so that their testimony is delivered seamlessly. Your client may not win an Oscar, but she will win over the jury!

Hollywood's Influence on Jurors

Before a big audition, it is standard for actors to book a session with an acting coach like myself to help them prepare, rehearse the audition, and work on being truthful under pressure. You need to be the acting coach for your client. This chapter will cover the most basic tools to teach your client how to be truthful and believable in the heart of the moment. Role-play and practice are the best and most efficient ways to achieve these skills. The more unprepared the witness is, the worse his performance.

Amazingly, today's jurors often base what they expect in court from Hollywood's portrayal of a courtroom. Think of all the TV shows that are set in law offices or police shows where the lead characters end up testifying. Even modern films portray many scenes of a case unfolding and the process a character might experience in court. Let's not even get into what crime scene investigation shows have done to confuse the use of DNA evidence at trial.

Jurors these days are hard to win over. They demand a performance, and they distrust everyone from the start. Maybe they feel it's the closest they will ever get to being on a reality TV show. If one witness is calm, confident, and prepared, and the opposing witness is quiet, nervous, and low-key, who do you think the jury will believe more? Despite the evidence they may have been presented with, the jurors will side with the individual who put on a better show and who told the story best.

There are eight important ways to best prepare your witness before the big show. We'll cover each one in detail throughout the chapter so you can play the role of the much-needed acting coach for your witness. These tips require rehearsal, at least a week before your witness will take the stand. Do you think "Phantom of the Opera" opened on Broadway without any rehearsal? This is the big show, and your client needs big rehearsals to give her a chance to practice her testimony without hesitation, in a trustworthy way. Unlike with a Broadway musical, there is only one shot to get it right. There are no repeat performances or Sunday matinees.

Before we begin, here is an important fact to consider. For an actor, a major source of stress occurs when the cast cannot move into the theater space until the very last minute, giving them almost no rehearsal time in the space where they will perform the show. Often, your client may feel the same. Give him the chance to meet you at the location where the deposition will be, or at the courthouse where the trial will take place, so he is familiar with how to get there, available parking, and the type of space you will be in. It can even be calming to know where the bathroom, water fountains, and snack machines are. This way, on the big day, there will be a sense of familiarity and comfort.

Bring the witness into the courtroom before the hearing. Have her sit in every seat in the house for perspective, such as the witness chair, your chair, the juror's box, and the back of the room. Here is where you can cover how loudly they need to speak to be heard, and the size and sound dynamic of the room, in case you have to speak more clearly due to high ceilings.

Eight Top Tips for Coaching Your Witness

1. How You Say It Is Just as Important as What You Say

Opposing council and juries are looking for any excuse to place a label on your witness. Remind witnesses when answering questions to answer in complete words—instead of saying "Uh-huh" or "Uh-uh," they should say "Yes," or "Yes, sir/ma'am," etc. Remind them that every word they say is being taken down by a court reporter, so have them think of this experience as a book someone may read. They need to express themselves as clearly and simply as possible. This advice also goes for nodding or shrugging. Remind them to speak distinctly and slowly so that the reporter can transcribe their testimony accurately.

Instruct your witness to avoid absolutes in his speech. "I never" or "I always" have a way of coming back to haunt you. Just ask Bill Clinton. Some people, when under stress, will make jokes. When my good friend, who is bald, was diagnosed with cancer, he looked right at the doctors and said, "Does this mean I will lose my hair?" Being doctors, they were immune to humor, and started going into the details of chemotherapy. (Okay, I'm sure some doctors have a sense of humor. I just haven't met any of them.) Sometimes jokes are okay, but *not* on the stand. Your witnesses must show that they take their oath very seriously. Finally, instruct witnesses to avoid even the mildest obscenity and avoid any reference that could be derogatory to any sex, ethnic origin, race, or religion. Again, nerves will take over, so if in meetings you catch witnesses making comments like this or using swear words as a way to describe things, give them time to absorb the fact that their words need to be chosen carefully so as to not offend the jury.

> **Quick Tip 8.1: Timing Is Everything**
>
> As you are entering the courtroom, never tell witnesses, "Now, don't swear or say anything offensive." This is going to freeze them up completely, as they fear that every other word that comes out of their mouth will be deemed inappropriate or offensive to the jury. You must tell witnesses this warning *at least a week before the big day* to give them time to practice eliminating those words from their everyday speech.

Advise witnesses to listen to the questions presented by opposing counsel very carefully. Make sure they understand the question. Tell them not to be afraid to say that they do not understand the question. There is nothing wrong with having the examiner repeat the question.

There is a great acting exercise, based on the Meisner method of acting, called Repetition. This will help develop the ability to really listen to the question or statement directed to you. When actors are working on a scene, they will look at the other actor and repeat any question, as if trying to understand or absorb what is being said to them. For example, if opposing counsel asks your client, "What time did you arrive at the south-side mini-mart that evening?," he should repeat, "What time did I get to the mini-mart?"

Clients may come across as slightly off-balance if they repeat every question out loud before their response. However, this can be done internally, in their mind, to offer a few valuable benefits: 1) It gives witnesses time to think about how they will answer in a calm and truthful way, and 2) it ensures that witnesses understand the question. If they don't, they can ask for clarification. This will help them avoid being tricked into saying something they did not mean to say. Here are some examples from a Meisner exercise.

1. "You're laughing." "I'm laughing?" "You're laughing!" "Yes, I'm laughing."
2. "You're staring at me." "I'm staring at you?" "You admit it?" "I admit it"
3. "I don't like it." "You don't like it?"
4. "You don't care?" "I don't care?" "That's right, you don't care." "It's true, I don't care."

Above all, instruct your witnesses to not answer a question if they do not understand what is being asked. It is up to the examiner to ask intelligible, unambiguous questions. If the examiner is being vague, there is no need for your witness to help him. A witness may chime in with "Do you mean A or do you mean B?" This can be disastrous. Train witnesses to simply state that they don't understand the question and force the examiner to rephrase the question or withdraw it.

> **Exercise 8.1: Confuse Your Client in Rehearsal**
>
> The best way to help your witness master saying "I don't understand the question" is role-playing. Ask a long, convoluted question to your witness in rehearsal and see if he tries to answer it. If he responds with something like "Do you mean was I drunk when I was driving, or drunk when I got home?," here is a teaching opportunity. Teach witnesses to never offer any information on a confusing question. Give them a chance to practice this with you. There is a strange instinct to be helpful and to please when in the witness box. This must be obliterated in your rehearsal. Positive feedback goes a long way. Give them praise when they catch a confusing question and respond accurately.

2. Compound Questions

In rehearsal, advise your witness to listen for compound questions. A compound question is two questions in one: "Did you see your brother hit the man, and was the man drunk?" The answer to that question could be yes and no. A witness must never get duped into answering compound questions. Your witness, or you as the attorney, must ask the examiner to split it into two parts if this type of question occurs.

Again, you have to practice this in rehearsal; this is the best way to ensure that your witness won't be tricked into giving a compromising answer to a compound question. Train her to say, "I'm sorry, I didn't understand the question." Ask compound questions about every three questions into your rehearsal so your witness feels confident that she can spot a compound question.

Finally, be sure to train your witness to pay particular attention to introductory clauses preceding questions. Leading questions are often preceded by statements that are either half-truths or facts that you know to be true. It is easy for a witness to answer a question but not have truly heard the question in its entirety. This situation is similar to what actors experience in a high-pressure audition environment.

For performers, a magical, weird hearing loss occurs when they are receiving direction or feedback. After an audition on camera, the director may say, "That was great, Laura. This time, can you try it a little angrier at the end, and maybe start the scene a bit flirtier?" So I, in an adrenalin-spiked daze, say, "Sure!" But when that camera rolls, my mind has gone blank. Wait, did he say more flirty or less? Did he want me to be angry? And what was I supposed to do at the end? Smile? Hit him? Oh, crap! (All of this is going on as I am performing my scene.)

Your client may be in the same hearing-impaired, adrenalin-warped time zone. Don't let him agree to something that is not true, or a half-truth. He may be embarrassed to admit that he did not hear the beginning of the question, was not completely listening, but has now responded to just the end of the sentence because it seemed like an answer he could offer because it's the last thing he heard or remembered.

3. Truth: You CAN Handle the Truth!

Lying under oath is bad for your witness, bad for your case, and bad for the impression it will make on the jury. Even if the witness feels upset over having to answer a particular question, being open, truthful, and honest are the keys to your witness's success. It's a lot easier to explain a truth than to explain a lie.

In improvisation, there is a basic rule that says "Don't ask questions." Asking a question in a scene just means you know what you want to happen, and you are forcing it on others. For example, you may say, "Did you break your leg?", and the person in the scene says "No," but you have already started reacting as if they did, because you have a funny idea for a couple on a first date and one has a broken leg. Similar to improvisation, there are *no true questions asked in a trial;* there is always an assumed answer. Here is where role-play comes in, and your client will benefit from role-playing this scenario of being asked a question that he or she does not want to answer.

> ### Quick Tip 8.2: Pull the Band-Aid Off in Rehearsal
>
> Sometimes taking a band-aid off in our mind is worse than the real thing. Your witness feels this concern over big questions he may not know how to answer in the best light. Say to him, "Is there a topic or type of question you are afraid will be asked when we are at trial?" Listen carefully to his response, and then role-play how he will answer. Don't be afraid to get aggressive or emotionally heightened in your role-play as the examiner. You can emphasize that although the intention of opposing council will or should not be to harass or pressure a witness in an inappropriate or aggressive way, witnesses need to know what it feels like to be under the heat of questioning. It is a best-case scenario if the rehearsal with you was 100 times more intense or intimidating than the actual court proceeding, and this will also make your client feel prepared and confident in your ability to show him in the best light possible. As they say in the theatre, "Bad dress rehearsal, good show!"

4. **Put the Dress in Dress Rehearsal**

Unfortunately, a jury will often be tempted to judge a book by its cover. Don't have the moment where your witness shows up to court in flip-flops, a tank top (which shows off her tattoos nicely), and her favorite sparkly nose ring. When you have your rehearsal at the courthouse as suggested above, ask her to wear the outfit that you have agreed upon in advance. Also, always have a few sets of decent clothing options tucked away at your office for emergencies. Often, a client's favorite or lucky shirt may be what causes the jury to dislike or not trust them.

Just like you, your witness is playing a role, so what costume will demonstrate this role? Do you want him to come across as professional? Then he needs to be in a crisp, clean suit. If she is playing the role of mistreated artist, then have her wear some of the handmade jewelry she sells. Similar to an audition, we want the audience to be focusing on what the witness has to say instead of how they managed to squeeze into a hot-pink sparkly halter top. There is a saying in acting: You never want your outfit to be more interesting than you are. This goes for your witness as well.

Let's say I am auditioning for the role of a street kid. Is it smart for me to wear my favorite diamond necklace or my wedding ring? Absolutely not! I need to dress the part. Before I was married, when I was auditioning for a lot of commercials, I went to the store and bought a cheap wedding ring specifically for the times I was auditioning for the role of a mom. And it worked! If the casting director can see you as a mom without having to work very hard or use her imagination, you already have won half the battle. You may get a few complaints from your witness if you ask her to make small changes to her appearance, or be told that if she takes out the piercing it may close up, since she just got it last night. If she says this, please refer to the next point below.

5. Pre-show Routines

Encourage your witness to wake up on the day of the trial and stick to his usual routine up to the time of the court proceeding. Many actors will do weird and wacky things the day or week before a big audition in some sort of subconscious self-sabotage, like get a new (terrible) haircut, start an aggressive exercise plan, stop eating dairy, or wax their eyebrows for the first time.

Witnesses may be tempted to drink with friends the night before the trial, change their look, get a new haircut or a tattoo, break a leg skiing, etc. Remind them to get plenty of rest the night before. When they wake up the day of the trial, tell them to eat a nutritious, well-balanced breakfast; they will need the physical and mental energy during the proceeding. Warn them not to eat a heavy meal, like the Denny's Grand Slam breakfast. This may seem obvious to you, but not to clients. The squirming in their seat from indigestion will make it look like they are hiding something or are uncomfortable.

Tell your client or witnesses that they are now on stage 24/7 as witnesses in this proceeding. There is a funny but true story about an actor on his way to an important audition for a TV show in Albuquerque. He was running late and was speeding to get to the audition on time. Right in front of him was a woman who was also speeding but seemed to be cutting him off at every turn and lane change. The actor finally was able to get ahead of the car and shouted out his window, "Nice blinker, asshole!" as he drove by. As he pulled into the parking lot, he noticed the same car was right behind him. The actor panicked, as he assumed the driver followed him to initiate a fight. But she quickly ran into the same building where the audition was being held. And guess who was sitting behind the camera, casting the role for the TV show? The same lady he yelled at on the road. Shockingly, he did not get the part. Funny story for us, but this was a terrible experience for him.

Similarly, you must instruct your witness that she is being watched at all times, even before taking the stand. When your witness is driving to court, chatting with her mother on her cell phone, and smoking a cigarette in front of the courthouse, or even chatting to someone in the bathroom, she is potentially being watched by someone involved in her case. Witnesses must carry themselves in a respectful way, even when they are in the bathroom, because you never know who is in the stall next to you. If this seems boring or stifling to your witness, tell them this is what Angelina Jolie and Brad Pitt go through every day of their lives. The paparazzi are always there, waiting for them to slip up.

6. I Did Not Say That

If you are able to coach your witness to say two things, these are the most important. Let's start with "I did not say that." A witness must not let an examiner put words in her mouth. If witnesses do not agree with a characterization of their prior testimony, they must say so. Advise them to simply state that they do not agree. "I did not say that" is a perfect answer.

The response "I did not say that" must be practiced, because it can feel aggressive or defensive for a witness to say. Have your witness imagine that the examiner is a three-year-old who is trying to put words in his mouth. No need to be angry; just be calm and matter-of-fact.

> **Toddler:** "But Mom! That's not fair—you said I could have a cookie as soon as we got home!"
> **Mom:** "I did not say that, Billy. I said you could have a cookie after you cleaned up your room, which you have not done. And by the way, you were an accident."

Advise the witness that she is in control and must stand up to any attacks from the examiner. Help your witness recognize clues that the examiner is setting her up unfairly. If your witness can sense that the examiner is trying to pin her down to facts that are not entirely true, talk to her about how to qualify her answer. Also remind her that she has you there to back her up should opposing counsel violate any procedural rules.

Exercise 8.2:
Deflect an Overstatement by the Examiner

Examiners will often try to overstate your witness's testimony. They may say, "Didn't you say that you never did that?" Train witnesses to say, "I did not say that, what I said was_____," and then qualify their answer. This is where extreme focus is of value, so they must remember what they actually said. Of course, remind your witness that it's always easy to remember the truth; wishy-washy excuses or confusing stories are harder to recall.

7. Pause and Think before Answering Every Question to Set Your Own Tempo

This trick will help witnesses to analyze questions and then answer. Have them repeat the question in their mind. The more they do this, the more it becomes second nature, and the easier it is for your witness. If they answer immediately, they are allowing the examiner to dictate the tempo of the questioning. It is especially important when you see witnesses getting tired or feeling under pressure. Tell them not be embarrassed by taking the time they may need to answer a question. If the examining attorney comments on the record that they are taking too much time, they can simply say that they want to be sure their answer is accurate.

For actors, too much untamed adrenalin can ruin an audition or performance. Adrenalin affects your brain as well as your muscles. The good news is that this energy can been harnessed and used for good with practice and patience. For your clients, the major effect of adrenalin is how they experience the *passage of time*. Most often, new actors will experience intense nervousness, dry mouth, shaking hands, speaking too quickly, or nervous tics, like fiddling with a necklace or wringing their hands. These are "tells" you can expect witnesses to make when they feel conscious of time passing slowly. It's your job to teach them to not get sucked into the adrenalin time warp. Many of these fidgets will actually make your client look less reliable on the stand.

Not only is a calm moment of silence important for clients to gather their thoughts on the question, but it also helps the room hear what is being said. Moments of silence are the most powerful moments in film acting. Actors call them nonverbal reactions; you call them moments of silence. Either way, use them and teach your clients to use them. Three seconds to the listener is absolutely appropriate, but to witnesses this will feel like an eternity. Train them to stop, breathe, and then respond; remind them that they are in control.

8. Do Not Volunteer Information

This tip absolutely must be practiced in rehearsal. Explain to witnesses that their job is to answer the question put to them—nothing more, nothing less. They must be trained to answer only the question asked, not what they suspect the examiner is trying to get at. Often it will feel like a casual friendship or conversation is happening, but witnesses must remember, this is business. They have to answer the question accurately but as respectfully and briefly as possible. There is no need for a witness to try to explain why he or she did or said a particular thing. This is not a social occasion at happy hour, it is a legal proceeding.

In rehearsals, try to be buddies with the witness when you act as the opposing attorney, then nail him with a question you have been planning that may tempt him to volunteer more information than what was asked of him. See if your witness falls into the trap of offering more in an effort to be helpful or to clarify. If he falls for this trick, stop and advise him of what just happened. Then ask the question again in rehearsal and ensure that he responds appropriately, while maintaining an air of professionalism and simplicity.

A similar tactic you can rehearse with your witness is when she is asked fuzzy or vague questions or her beliefs on a certain topic. Again, the need to be helpful may override the fact that the witness has answered a question she is actually confused by. If you have trained her well, she will respond with "Can you rephrase or repeat the question?" or "I don't understand what you are asking me."

You may see the examiner pull out his best acting skills and act confused or surprised when your witness answers a particular question. Don't let your witness be fooled by this performance! If the witness is looking at a confused face, advise him that there is no need to clarify what he has said. The examiner is not the witness's confused and caring friend. The witness must not be lulled into that type of thinking despite the conversation or light tone the examiner may use. The examiner's job is solely to get testimony that is damaging to the witness and helpful to his case. In rehearsals, after your witness makes a statement, look at him with a furrowed brow and a lightly surprised look on your face. Look at him expectantly, as if he is going to say more, and nod. See if your witness falls for it. If he does fall for it and offers more information, review the fact that there is no need to ever volunteer more information when he has already answered the question. Nothing more needs to be said. The more witnesses practice this idea, the more confident they will be about censoring their instinct to explain or clarify.

Closing Argument

Practice all eight of these scenarios using role-play, and see if your client has mastered the art of pausing, saying "I did not say that," "I don't understand the question," and being concisely honest. Use aggressive body language and vocal tone with clients when you play the role of the examiner or get into their personal space. Anything that they may be likely to experience on the big day must be rehearsed. One hour of rehearsal can mean a victory at trial, so it's worth it. Your witness may not "win" the trial, but you can be assured he or she won't be what cost you the trial.

Chapter 9

Delivering Closing Arguments as Monologues

Opening Statement: An Attorney's Time to Shine

Actors consider monologues to be the ultimate showcase of their talents. This is their opportunity to use charisma and creativity to get the role. Closing arguments provide attorneys one last chance to plead their case to the jury. The successful attorney will have set the jury up for this closing argument from the very beginning of the trial, so that all of the reason, passion, and sympathy of the jury will be primed to fall into place at that final crucial moment of deliberation.

Most litigators would hardly call their closing arguments exciting, so why are films set in the courtroom infinitely more exciting than the real courtroom? Actors know how to prepare a monologue to be impactful on their audience. Attorneys already know how to draft a solid closing argument, but they are not taught the skills required to drive home their argument by way of delivery. Actors have been honing this skill since junior high drama club. A closing argument is nothing more than a monologue, the staple of the dramatic actor.

112 CHAPTER 9

The art of creating and perfecting your closing argument is best approached as an actor approaches a monologue. We will use the skills that actors have in their back pockets to demonstrate and nail down a closing argument that will seal the deal.

Concentration

"Concentration" is the term most often used to describe what the actor does to involve himself in an imaginary dramatic situation. The word *concentration* is almost interchangeable with the word *technique*. Concentration is the key to what an actor does while studying, rehearsing, auditioning, or performing.

For me, concentration is a tool to avoid being thrown off when I am affected by how my audience is responding. If I am in the middle of a big monologue from *The Importance of Being Earnest*, and some guy in the front row is unwrapping a mint as slowly as he can (so as to not attract attention, which of course magnifies every crinkle of the damn wrapper), it's easy for the me to lose my concentration and mentally move to the other side of the stage. This is emotionally judging yourself and the experience, which is exactly where you *don't* want to be in the middle of a monologue or closing argument. You have to use all of your concentration to stay in the moment and maintain the momentum you have created.

> **Quick Tip 9.1: Concentration Exercise**
>
> Grab a newspaper or magazine and memorize the first five sentences of an article. Once you have the paragraph memorized, attempt to recite it under different distracting scenarios, e.g., with the TV blasting, while making the bed, or while doing jumping jacks. This is a great way to hone your level of focus and concentration, and can be done with material you have to present for work or social situations.

Make It Personal

If you aren't truly relating to the "characters" in your closing argument, it can be a real sticking point. You haven't had the exact life experiences that your client has had, but you may have experienced something that would give rise to similar emotions. Take a minute and make this story personal to you, and it will make all the difference in the world. It is much easier to pull events from real life, something that means something to you. If your wife, husband, or partner has ever been sick, wronged, or in danger, you can relate. You may have to think hard about events in your life and spend some time quietly thinking of the details of your case, but with very little effort you will be able to find an experience you have had that is comparable to the experience your client has had or is experiencing.

Sense Memory

Sense memory is a powerful tool. As human beings, we have years of powerful memories that can be used to develop a solid closing argument. Most of our poignant memories are not absent thoughts, they are sense memories. Think of the moments from a great vacation that stick out: the smell of fresh mangoes for breakfast, the cold sting of the wind on your face when you went snowshoeing in Canada, the roar of the crowd when your college football team won the game no one ever thought they could win. These are all sense memories. Those images are never lost. When your sense memory is finely tuned, you can recall special experiences you have had, and also see, smell, taste, touch, and hear all the little details in your mind.

So, How Can We Use Sense Memory in Our Closing Arguments?

By relating to your client's past experiences or moments that are part of the story or case, you can re-create the experience, the pain, the confusion, the betrayal, the success, and the wrongdoings. You can depend upon the fact that your reaction to that experience will be an honest, believable, interesting human reaction, and not an indicated or demonstrated reaction. After that, the jury is with you 100 percent.

How to Fine-Tune Your Sense Memory Skills

As a performer, you can make your sense memories come alive inside of you or you can project them outside of you. For most people, there is a screen just behind their eyes where they can see specific moments from their past. This is called the "mind's eye." With practice, you can place that screen anywhere outside of yourself that you want it. You will be able, for example, to look out over the jury or into the judge's eyes and see a view you have seen from a mountaintop. This technique is what all famous film actors use in close-up shots. They are looking beyond the camera to those images, and their eyes tell the whole story.

On an interesting note, anytime there is a shot in a movie of an actor looking at a mirror, there is almost never a mirror there at all, because it would reflect the camera and equipment. So when an actor fixes her hair or puts on lipstick in a mirror, give her kudos for doing this all from sense memory skills. She is most likely staring at a blank wall, into the camera, or at the back of the wardrobe woman's head. Similarly, there probably isn't a mirror behind the jury box, reflecting your image back to you (unless your courthouse doubles as a disco on Saturday nights, which would be awesome).

> **Exercise 9.1: Developing Your Sense Memory Skills**
>
> Here is an exercise to help you fine-tune your sense memory skills in order to apply them to your closing argument. Sit up straight in a chair and relax. Close your eyes and remember an object or an outdoor place where you have gone in your past to relax (think a hammock in Hawaii, your parents' backyard, or a bench at the local park). See the image projected behind your eyes. Open your eyes and let the image project itself in front of you. If the image is nowhere to be seen, just close your eyes and restore the image on your interior screen. Relax, open your eyes, and see the same image projected out in front of you.

Don't be afraid to tap into your other senses to explore past memories as well: the touch of a loved one's hands on yours, the taste of a kiss on your mouth, the smell of cologne or perfume from a first date, the sound of a best friend's voice over the phone. The key to sense memory is relaxation, and when you are relaxed you are in control.

The Inner Monologue

Before we move to the monologue/closing argument that you present at trial, we need to take a moment to understand the power of an *inner* monologue. What an actor's character wants or needs can also become an inner monologue. And so, what you or your client wants can be *your inner monologue*. The inner monologue helps keep the focus on your intention, or what you want from the jury.

Imagine if the sentence you are saying is "You've been a doctor at this hospital for twenty years, correct?" That is what comes out of your mouth, but your inner monologue is saying, "So, there is no reason why this error should have happened, based on your experience and tenure at this hospital. You should have known better." Do you see the difference?

There is more impact to your words when there is an inner dialogue that occurs at the same time that you speak. Here is an example that actors might use. In a scene with an ex-boyfriend, I may have the line "Pass the ketchup, please" but my inner monologue is "I want to make love to you so badly, let's get back together!" What a powerful difference. Now the script has come alive. You need to apply the same inner monologue technique for your closing argument, turning mechanical words into a passionate expression of thought.

> **Quick Tip 9.2:**
>
> **Tune Into Your Ongoing Inner Monologue**
>
> We are constantly running an inner monologue as we go through the day. Try to spend an afternoon noticing all the thoughts that run through your mind that you do not verbalize out loud, like "I'm starving," "I can't believe the FedEx guy is late again," "Did I forget to call my dad on his birthday?," and "Wow, I never noticed how dirty my glasses are."

When we have an inner monologue, our eyes change as we are computing this information. Attorneys can use an inner dialogue to send a secondary message to the jury without saying word. This is a subtle and powerful way to drive home your point with the jury, once you realize how you are already performing this trick all through the workday.

Know Your Intention

In order to have a powerful closing argument, you need to apply the trick that actors use to make their monologues spring off the page with real and true emotions. This trick is called "intention." Behind everything we say is an intention. What is it we intend to convey with our words? The words themselves carry meaning, but behind the words is the true intent of the speaker. What is it you are hoping to accomplish with your comments? As you study your closing argument, look for opportunities to add an intention that make sense, either for every section or on a specific thought. When your words are used as an action to fulfill the intention, the words will come alive. They will sound like the verbal expression of a purposeful human being, not a bored, mechanical litigating machine just relaying information. The jury wants to be entertained, fascinated, pulled, and convinced. Here are some examples of intentions:

1. To brag
2. To celebrate
3. To discover
4. To frighten
5. To humiliate
6. To impress
7. To make fun of
8. To pay attention to
9. To pick a fight
10. To please
11. To praise
12. To support
13. To try to remember
14. To prove

Are you getting excited at the possibilities yet? This is fun stuff; this is a clear intention you are working toward. What you do as attorneys is battle it out and see which professional can tell the best story. You now you have the tools to dominate and succeed.

Try the following sentence out loud, with a few of the above intentions as the force behind it.

"You've been a doctor at this hospital for twenty years, correct?"

Are you starting to see the power of words when paired with intentions? Now, let's add even more power to this tool with attitude.

Attitude

What attitude do you want to adopt when performing your closing argument? As we now know, your point of view will be reflected in your demeanor, inflections, and tone of voice. The tone you use when talking to your witness will be very different from your tone when speaking to the jury, judge, or opposing counsel.

One of the worst things an actor can do in a monologue is play it safe. It is the same for attorneys. If you can't "name your attitude," there probably is nothing there at all other than word vomit. Don't supply word vomit! It's the big show! Obviously, you will use your discretion, depending on whether the case is very serious (death, injury, etc). But if you have no attitude behind your words, the audience or jury is left confused about your intention. Here is a list of attitudes that we can pair with our intentions.

1. Angry
2. Condescending
3. Defeated
4. Deflated
5. Emphatic
6. Hopeful
7. Happy
8. Incredulous
9. Parental
10. Snooty
11. Surprised
12. Understanding

So, to tie it all together, you may have an intention of "to discover" with an attitude of being "emphatic" if you want to drive home the point that the doctor made an error that all his colleagues agree never should have happened, based on his 20-plus years of experience in the field.

Practice saying the sentence again, pairing different intentions and attitudes from the list:

"You've been a doctor at this hospital for twenty years, correct?"

> **Exercise 9.2: Attitude Party Game**
>
> Either on your own or with friends (this is lots of fun with friends, so grab one or more for this game), write down on little pieces of paper all the kinds of attitudes one might display (use the above list for suggestions, and add your own ideas). Fold up the papers and put them in a pile. One by one, each player must select a paper and act out the attitude on it without actually saying the word. Other players must call out the attitude they think the performer is showing until the attitude is guessed correctly. It's like charades, but you can talk! If no one seems to be guessing your attitude, take time to think about the disconnect between your attitude and your body language. What are you trying to show? As you play more rounds, you will get better and better at switching attitudes on a dime.

Faith or Fear?

Which do you bring to your closing argument?

Actors often will go from buying the whole bar shots after they booked a huge commercial to eating crackers for two weeks straight until the next gig comes in. Performers know that when they get an opportunity to showcase their skills, they have to do it right the first time. No one likes stale crackers. Having trust in yourself and your skills is a necessary anchor in the monologue performance process. Directors can smell desperation and self-consciousness a mile away.

One day, when I was a young actress living in Toronto, my agent called me and told me I had an audition in 45 minutes. I was beyond agitated. I already had plans to go with my girlfriends to the beach for some fun in the sun, and they were literally waiting for me to hop into the car. I quickly threw a summer dress over my bikini and we all drove over to the audition. The audition was for a small but wonderful local theater production. Due to the fact that I had no time to prepare or research the play, I had no choice but to just go in, have fun, and blow it off as a way to just work on my monologue. I boldly walked in, performed my monologue with wild abandon (it was a great monologue where a woman lost her mind in the middle of a sales pitch), had a blast because I had no time to be nervous, and happily walked out the door when it was over. I couldn't have cared less if I got the role, because that day Hawaiian Tropic oil and beach volleyball were calling my name. Guess what? I got the role.

So, give yourself *permission to tell a story.* In whatever way makes the most sense for you, you have to find ways to access your higher self, so you can let go of lower, insecure, fear-based energies. Learn how to breathe deeply and properly, and to connect with your body.

After the successful experience I had at the audition, I found that simply wearing a bikini under my clothes reminds me of the confidence and detachment I had at that audition, and I still use this trick to this day to get myself to the point of power, relaxation and faith that I am indeed, "The Bomb." So, what tricks do you have?

Another trick I use is to imagine I have shown up on the big day in a limo, or that my private jet is out back that will whisk me to the Greek Islands once my work here is done. Use your imagination, and find a way to bring faith, not fear, to your closing argument. Remember, what we do is supposed to be fun—at least once in a while!

Stage Fright

Any actor who studies improvisation is familiar with the queen of improvisational training, Viola Spolin. Spolin states that stage fright is a *fear of judgment.* She states the actor is afraid of criticism, of being ridiculous, of forgetting lines, etc. So many attorneys I work with have the same fears, especially in closing arguments, when all eyes are on them. They may harbor some fears about their appearance, but more important, they may be concerned that what is coming out of their mouth may not be considered intelligent, or artful, or even correct.

Similar to Viola's extensive work filled with exercises and techniques using improvisation as a tool for success, the exercises in this book will help to solve all the common problems that attorneys face when speaking in public almost before they arise, because actors know what it is like to stand in front of people and risk it all. Your reputation, your success, and your clean underwear are on the line. The true goal of any public demonstration is to showcase your best possible performance and have confidence in yourself.

Obvious but Often Missed Questions to Ask Yourself

Once you have written your closing argument, here are five questions to ask yourself before you work on becoming very familiar with your material:

1. Do I start with a bang?
Actors know to choose and piece together a monologue that has a strong first beat, or moment. We will start with a powerful first line of "So, what? You've never met a hooker before?" Anything surprising and attention-getting will do the trick. An attorney must do the same. The first sentence of your closing argument must grab the jurors with a hook or a strong statement that will compel them to continue listening. Be sure to show your enthusiasm in the case as you lay out why the jury should file in your favor. You are setting the tone for your entire closing argument. Here's another way to think about this: Did you know that most casting directors decide if an actor is good within the first five seconds? Five seconds! Those first five seconds for an attorney must also be attention-grabbing and full of passion.

2. What is my goal for the jurors?
Every actor who prepares a monologue always asks three key questions: What do I want? What's in my way? What will I do to get it? These questions force us to be clear about our intentions in the monologue and to actively find ways to achieve and drive toward our goal. This commitment to our goals also helps bring the piece to life, instead of performing a safe and boring regurgitation of words on a page.

Use these same powerful tools for your closing argument. What do you want from the jury specifically? We know in the grand scheme of things that you want the jury to agree with you and to feel good about the conclusion they have made. Be very clear what you want from the jury, and state this in words. Then ask yourself, "What is blocking me from my goal, and how am I going to remove this block?" Here you can mention your case strengths and identify the major problems with your opponent's argument. You can even challenge its weaknesses point by point to get what you want. This will shape your strategy into a powerful, forward-moving argument, perfectly molded and executed.

3. Am I being mindful of my time?
Many times a monologue must be no more than two minutes long. The actor who gambles and refuses to shorten his piece from two and a half minutes is about to get a rude awakening. At two minutes exactly, some casting directors will say, "Okay, thanks," and cut you off. The actor will cry, "But I haven't gotten to the good part yet!" Well, lesson learned. Don't wait until the last 30 seconds for the "good part." Be good right away, and maintain this until the end. You likely will have an allotted amount of time for your closing argument as well, so be sure to get in as much detail as possible based on the time you have.

4. Am I clear and organized?
If an actor will be using a picture frame or a chair in their monologue, you can bet he has checked 20 times before the audition that everything is in its place. You must do the same. Do you have everything in hand you want to refer to? Are your facts organized into a clear and concise structure? Do you remember which witness's testimony you will refer to in particular? An attorney must be sure to organize his argument and present it as a logical discussion with the jury. The jury is your eye line, your audience, and your listeners. The easiest way to be clear about your argument is to connect with them; offer eye contact, gestures, and, above all, be very clear that you firmly believe in your case.

5. Does the body of your closing argument build to a climax at the end?
A strong ending is vital to an actor's monologue. It must be completed with passion and focus so that when it's over you don't just

fade away and mumble "Well, that's it, that's the end." Use the climax of your piece as a way to connect the dots for the jury so that the jury knows you indeed are correct. Tie the closing together with the theme with which you began your opening statement. The final few moments of your closing argument must not be read or recited. It must be committed to memory so that you can execute a powerful, passionate last moment. The last thing you say will remain on the mind of the jury, so make a strong and persuasive choice for your last sentence.

Closing Argument

Once the above skills are mastered, the courtroom will forever become your own: your space, your time, your story. And when the curtain falls, or the case is resolved, the show will go on. You may not receive roses after a great courtroom performance (actors are even more egomaniacal than lawyers and need constant signs of approval and admiration, hence the roses), but you will leave the courtroom a little taller, all eyes on you, as if all the jurors are in a contented trance. That is a perfect closing argument. And that kind of success is enough to make you want to do it all over again every week.

Chapter 10

How to Take a Great Photo

Opening Statement

Inevitably, you will need to have a photo taken of you, whether it's for the company website or a head shot for business cards, corporate opportunities, Facebook, LinkedIn, or group social events. The photograph literally puts a "face" on your organization and your practice. Larger firms and companies put a lot of time and effort into their employee head shots and company pictures.

Think of images you've seen of CEOs from big corporations like Dell, Microsoft, and Google. The expression on their face, the body language, the clothes, the background, the colors—everything is designed to instill in us an impression about the company. None of these details are left to chance, and a professional photographer will be sure the shot looks perfect.

Most people dread having their photo taken. They are repulsed by the double chin, the weird shape their head seems to be, or their frozen facial expression. Sometimes a reflection in a mirror or glass can ruin your photo, even if you look great. This chapter will outline all the secret tips that actors and celebrities use to take the most flattering photo at all times and in every situation. You too can learn to be photogenic with these tips.

How to Pose for a Head Shot

For an actor, the 8" x 10" head shot acts essentially like a business card that is presented to casting directors, who decide whether a person has the right "look" for a particular part in a movie, TV show, or theatrical performance. It is not a "glamour shot." For attorneys, your headshot also serves as a way for people to remember you. Many business professionals I know will attach a photo to each contact they have in Outlook so they can remember what the person they met at last month's training looks like. These photos are most often pulled from the head shot found on your website or from an online lawyer directory. Your head shot is functional, both for others and yourself.

A good head shot is intended to market a person "as they are" (you should look your age, for example), but in as positive a light as possible. The photo should accentuate the subject's best qualities. A good head shot will often provide the viewer with a glimpse into the person's character. We will talk about what kind of character you may want to present in your head shot later in this chapter.

All attorneys play a role, and it is fun to decide what message you want your appearance to convey to your clients and competitors. A family law attorney specializing in domestic abuse cases will not want to convey the same message as a corporate attorney.

Actors know that when you are comfortable and enjoying what you are doing, it is much easier to project yourself to the camera in a confident, comfortable, and positive manner. You are also much more likely to feel comfortable experimenting with different looks, facial expressions, etc., which can lead to some unique, eye-catching, and outstanding head shots. Smiles are genuine, not fake, and expressions tend to be much more vibrant and alive.

How to Smile on Camera

We have all seen the adorable picture of the child, around age 7 or 8, who has not learned to smile on cue yet. When told to smile, the edges of their mouth slant up to the eyes, very tight, as if they have just tasted something terrible but are trying to hide it. Unfortunately, a lot of the attorney pictures I see look the same. It's obviously a fake smile, and it looks unnatural. You don't want to look like the guy on the left. On the right, he has achieved a natural smile.

There are two tricks I know of to smile on cue in a natural way:

Trick Number One— Imagine being punched in the gut.

The trick is to imagine that someone has just punched you in the stomach. As you imagine your stomach caving in from the blow, allow a smile to spread across your face. Yup, that surprise moment of impact as you smile will expel air from your mouth, helping you to relax and breathe. Also, it brings a sense of energy and aliveness to your shot. Of course, as the punch hits your stomach, you must laugh out loud a little, otherwise your face will show a painful blow to the gut. Try it right now!

Trick Number Two—Turn the camera into a friend.
The second way to have an authentic smile is to make the camera someone you love. It's really important not to look at the camera as if it's your enemy, ready to focus on all of your terrible traits, like the bags under your eyes or your patchy skin. I always look at the camera like it's my mom, because looking at my mom makes me happy. I imagine her smiling at me and we are having fun, laughing at a joke together. Sounds silly, but when you look at the camera like you are looking at a friend or loved one, your entire vibe changes to a more relaxed, open, and confident image. Plus, looking at a friend makes it way easier to connect. Your eyes are looking at an energy source that is also offering love back to you. It's not just you alone having to do all the work, because your mom, or best friend, or wife, or anyone special in your life, is smiling back at you.

Should I Try to Show My Personality in a Head Shot?

Yes, we want to see you and your personality in the picture. But this is still a business head shot. Your head shot is a marketing tool, and you should always be thinking about how to best market yourself. Like it or not, you are selling yourself. Don't be a fashion model. Avoid flipping your hair, leaning your chin on your hand, or using any kind of prop. I suppose if you're a judge you might get away with a gavel, but come on, really? The people who look at your head shot online want to see a straight-to-camera head shot, meaning eyes right to camera. They don't want to see you being cute or trying to look like a rock star, they want to see *you*. A successful head shot shows you in a moment of comfort and confidence with yourself. It is as simple as that.

The Day of the Shoot

For women, I always suggest getting your hair and makeup professionally done for a head shot. The makeup you wear every day to the office may be a bit too dark or a bit too plain in a photo. It will look overdone or washed out, or the colors you have chosen will look poor. Bring a few wardrobe choices, and make sure everything is clean and pressed. Solid colors will look better in the shot, and avoid fabric made of shiny or iridescent material.

I will assume if you are getting a head shot for business that you have hired a professional photographer. Don't ask your friend Bill, who takes good photos of garden gnomes with his digital camera. You need a professional, and it's worth every penny. A good place to start looking is a photographer who takes actors' head shots. There are even photographers who specialize in head shots and company photos for lawyers.

The Eyes Are Your Secret Weapon to a Great Head Shot

Across the board, in every kind of photo taken of you, your eyes tell the story and allow your head shot to convey a natural, confident attitude.

- Make your eyes come alive with active inner dialogue. We will cover that in more detail below.
- Know yourself to properly market yourself. Do you want to come across as a tough, no-nonsense attorney? Friendly and approachable? Extremely knowledgeable in your field? Old and distinguished? Young and peppy?
- Be comfortable and confident. Again, make the camera a great friend who sees all of your wonderful qualities and makes you feel a bit mischievous.
- Bring your personality to the shoot. Smile the way you smile, laugh the way you laugh. Give your best "Don't BS me" look if that's what you are known for.
- Wear what makes you feel your best. Avoid wild patterns, bright colors, and anything high fashion. You may choose to use this head shot for a really long time, and you want your look to be classic and flexible. You may decide down the road that you never want to wear a bow tie or clunky necklaces again, but your head shot freezes these choices in time.

- Make a connection to the camera. Lean toward it, not away from it! This is the most valuable trick I have learned from the hundreds of photos I have had taken of me as an actor. One very talented photographer had a table in front of me, and for every shot, I leaned way over onto the table, sometimes leaning on an arm or elbow, sometimes just my head toward the camera. He was always above me, standing up while I was sitting down. The effect was fantastic! I looked alive, engaged, and alert, and every shot was very flattering. It avoided any chance of a double chin, and also kept my energy level up. I felt like I was really trying to connect with the camera, almost as if I was leaning forward at a loud restaurant to hear my dinner companion's words.
- Relax your lips, jaw, face, and shoulders. Remember to breathe! Relaxation exercises must be done before you take a head shot. Do this in the bathroom, and right before shoot. Blow out of your lips and make horse noises and trills, and act like you are chewing a huge ball of peanut butter to stretch and relax your jaw. Roll your shoulders forwards and backwards to remove any tension. You can bet that tension in your neck and shoulders will absolutely show in your face.

Ways to Keep the Eyes Alive: Inner Dialogue

Although this is a trick that actors use when breaking down a scene, you can use the following as a technique to learn how to communicate with your eyes. An active inner dialogue during a photo shoot changes the photo from neutral and uncomfortable to confident, intriguing, and fun. Call up any Victoria's Secret model and ask her if she has an inner dialogue when she is posing. Oh, you don't have the phone number for any Victoria's Secret models? Something to put on your bucket list, I suppose! Here are some examples of inner dialogue thoughts, depending on the look or personality you want to show in your shot. Notice the active verbs (in capital letters) that help send the thought through your eyes and body.

- I want to EARN enough for a vacation home in Hawaii.
- I want to WIN my husband's admiration.
- I want to ELIMINATE conflict.
- I want to FASCINATE business owners.
- I want to ORGANIZE this mess the city is dealing with.
- I want to DESTROY unfair laws that affect small-business owners.
- I want to FOCUS my attention on your needs.
- I want to FIND a way to make this right.
- I want to TAKE CARE of your family.
- I want to DAZZLE my clients with enthusiasm.
- I want to FIGURE OUT a solution.
- I want to CONTAIN my outrage.
- I want to BELITTLE the company that wronged you.
- I want to IGNITE the crowd to riot.
- I want to PERSUADE Ann to kiss me.

Finding Actable Verbs

Another simple way to have an inner dialogue is to just think of actable verbs. I may say the word "dazzle," or "reassure," or "seduce," or "awaken" in my mind over and over. As I do this, my face will light up differently. My body comes alive and I am sending my message with every click of the camera.

Actable verbs are commonplace, gutsy activities. Here are a few to get your imagination going:

- Suppress, incite, inspire, hurt, enlighten
- Organize, crush, ensnare, explain, encourage
- Destroy, build, prepare, tease, lambaste
- Cheer up, mock, reassure, justify, convince
- Annihilate, ignite, get even, bombard, help
- Belittle, seduce, awaken, overwhelm

How to Pose for Group Photos

At social events, work parties, networking events, and more, your photo is being snapped and posted onto Facebook or the *State Bar Bulletin* before you can say, "Why didn't anyone tell me I had mustard on my shirt?" If you want to pose perfectly the way Hollywood does, I have three tips: spray tan, Spandex girdles, and starving yourself. For everyone else who enjoys eating and breathing, let's learn some tips you can apply the very next time your photo is snapped.

1. **Left shoulder forward.** Look thru any magazine or ad this weekend and see how many of the models put their left shoulder forward. The way the human eye reads and comprehends information is by looking from left to right, just like reading a book. If you put your left should forward a little, anywhere from two to five inches, two things will happen: First, you will automatically look slimmer; as it offers a bit of a side profile, showing your face in slight profile as well. Two, the photo will look less like a mug shot, as mug shots are taken head-on and are often not the way we look as we move through space. Place one foot toward the camera but put all your weight on your back foot. Jump up and try this pose right now.

2. **Push your head forward.** Use the same head trick as you will in your head shot. Be sure to pull your head forward slightly to minimize any appearance of a double chin, almost like a turtle sticking its head forward slightly. The instinct that most people have is the opposite, to pull back, because they feel self-conscious. This makes you look worse because you literally create a double chin for yourself.

3. **Get air under your armpits.** Hold your arms slightly away from your body. This keeps upper arm flab from flattening out and therefore appearing flabbier (much like thighs do when one sits on a chair). It also helps you look more relaxed.
4. **Posture.** Everyone looks better with good posture. Remember the idea of the two strings, pulling your head up and your chest up at a 45-degree angle across the room? Use this same trick in group photos. Also, don't feel you have to suck your gut in the to the point that you look like you are going to explode, but try to squeeze your stomach as tight as you can, like someone is going to come around the corner and punch you, and you are waiting for the blow. This will tighten things up nicely, and will help your spine stay erect and supported. (Plus, it's also like doing an abdominal crunch. More calories to spare for guacamole!)

5. **Distraction Technique.** The distraction technique works if you want to hide a certain aspect of your body by using a prop. Placing a purse, drink, binder, or other item on hand in front of your gut or the stain on your shirt will do the trick perfectly. It also looks quite lovely in photos, instead of sticking your arms by your side in an unnatural or stiff way.
6. **Shoot from Above.** Similar to the head shot, never let anyone take your picture from below. Casually say to the short photographer, "Hey, jump up on the chair so we don't chop off the tall people's heads!" This will make everyone look better. Or, just don't let short people take pictures at your social events. Tell them it's nothing personal. It's just business, baby.
7. **Inner Dialogue.** Use the same inner dialogue as you did with head shot, but the group shot can be more playful. Imagine that a very sexy person just walked into the room, and he is looking right at you, saying, "Wow, that person is gorgeous." Or imagine this is a group photo of lottery winners, of which you are one. Or imagine that you are the most popular person in the room and everyone wants a picture taken with you. I know, it sounds egomaniacal (that's how actors roll), but these tricks really work, and it's just more fun to have your photo taken when these thoughts are running through your head. You can also make eye contact with the camera at the last second, as opposed to staying in your frozen fake smile from before the photographer has even said, "Okay on one, two . . ." Have fun with it! If you think you are photogenic, then you will be. You have to believe it. If you can believe in Santa Claus or that the olives in your martini count as a daily serving of vegetables, you can handle this.

One Last Secret tip

Sometimes in a group shot a person will have the bright idea to yell out, "Okay everyone, say Keller, Williams and Stone [or another company name or funny phrase] on the count of three" as they are taking a photo. If you do this, I will fly to your event and punch you in the face. There is no better way to look like a freak than to be mouthing some weird phrase as the photo is being taken. I always just ignore this suggestion and look at the camera with my smile and inner dialogue. Most often, I am the only one who does not look like they have pepper up their nose. No one will know you didn't say the phrase, and you will look great in the photo. See how the guy on the left in this photo is the only one who doesn't look stupid? This should be you.

Closing Argument

Almost no one on earth thinks they are photogenic. Being photogenic is not an inherited trait, it is a developed skill. Sure, some people have more of a knack for it, but anyone can learn to take great photos. Before you hire a photographer to take your head shot, take a look online at some photographers' portfolios. There are photographers who specialize in attorney head shots. See what you like and what you don't like about how other attorneys have been photographed, and show up for your shoot armed with knowledge about how to look your absolute best.

Summation

Attorneys must be able to express themselves as effectively as possible. There is always an opportunity to practice your skills, whether at the company picnic or when you are buying milk. If you want to gain the audience's attention, keep it, and clearly relay your information, the use of vocal variety, improvisation, and storytelling will prove to be invaluable.

Finely tuned acting skills can also help you minimize the weaknesses of your cases and maximize the strengths. This book was designed to improve your public speaking skills so that others can more readily follow your arguments and be persuaded by them.

Have fun with the knowledge you now have! Initiate offering a toast at weddings, or tell a great joke at the next family dinner. The acting skills you are now developing can be applied to any situation, not just in the courtroom or in a business setting.

One more thing: If you are truly a passionate and skilled speaker, you will often give much more energy to an audience than you receive back. If you are exhausted after speaking in public, you know you have done it right.

By now you are probably thinking, "Wow, I would very much like to hire Laura Mathis to get her fantastic self down here to my firm and see all of this information in action!" If you are thinking that, you are correct. Good. I hope to see you soon!

Whether you are making us laugh, encouraging us to think more deeply, or just forcing opposing counsel to completely rethink the merits of his or her case, just have fun, stay focused, and be great. A life on the stage is not a far jump from the life of an attorney. Maybe I'll see you at an upcoming audition. With every successful speech, closing argument, or toast, you will enhance your power to perform even better in the future. I'll drink to that!

Index

A

acting classes for lawyers, value of, 82
Adler, Stella, 85
articulation, 25–26
  defined, 25
  development of, 26
  exercises for, 26
      vowel sound warm-up, 26
  factors involved in, 25
  tongue twister exercises, 26
attitude, closing arguments, importance in, 117
audience, control of, 3
audience issues. *Also see* juries, approaches to
  adapting to, 89–90
  engaging the audience, tips for, 89–90
  knowledge of, need for 36
  making a connection, 89

B

Belushi, John, 68
body language. *Also see* expression, nonverbal; eye contact; neutral position
  actions, messages conveyed by, 51–52
  confidence, conveying, 48
  different qualities, physical display of, 72
  emotions, key to, 49
  gaining control of, 49
  impact of, 45
  juries, reading, 36–38
  leading with your body exercise, 52
  moods, key to, 49
  observation exercise, 50
  personality, reflection of, 53
  understanding of subject matter, impact on, 48
breathiness as vocal problem, 21
breathing techniques, 22
  breath control, importance of, 22
  breathing exercises, 22
  throat, opening of, 23
      exercises for, 23
Buddha, 91

C

Chekhov, Michael, 85
Chubbuck, Ivana, 85
Clinton, Bill, 53, 100
character, 91–92. *Also see* role playing
  assuming, 39–42
      choices for, 40–42, 90
      exploring through breathing techniques, 42
  defining, 34
  role in storytelling, 90
  types of, 91–92
closing arguments, 111–12. *Also see* sense memory
  attitude, choice of, 117–19
      exercise for, 119
      options for, 118
  clarity, need for, 122
  concentration, 112
      exercise for, 112
      importance of, 112

creating, art of, 112
endings, options for, 122–23
faith vs. fear option, 119–20
goals, determining, 121
groundwork for, 111
inner monologue, application to, 115–16
intentions, determining, 116–17
    examples of, 117
openings, options for, 121
organization, need for, 122
stage fright, coping with, 120
time, awareness of, 122
concentration as key to closing argument, 112
confidence
    conveying through body language, 48–49
    lack of, 3
consonants, overexplosive, 20

D

depositions, 58–59. *Also see* witness questioning, techniques for; witnesses, relating to
    exercises for, 63
    location of, visiting, 98
    preparation for, 59
    purposes of, 58–59
        witness account, establishing, 59
        witness version, determining, 59
        witnesses, observing, 59
    rules regarding, review of, 58
    tempo of, dictating, 64
diction, poor, 20

E

emergencies, preparedness for, 3
entrances and exits, 14
    dance classes, usefulness of, 14
    graceful walk, impact of, 14
    posture, impact of, 14

Esposito, Giancarlo, 28
expression, nonverbal, 53–54. *Also see* eye contact
    action, suitability of, 53
    gestures, 53–54
        control of, 53
        matching with facial expressions, 54
    neutral position, role in, 53
    responses, natural, 53
eye contact, 54–55
    familiarity with material, importance of, 54
    improvisation, importance in, 77
    purpose of, 54
    responding to audience mood, 55
    techniques for, 55

F

Fallon, Jimmy, 60
Farley, Chris, 68
Farrell, Will, 91
Fey, Tina, 68

G

gestures, 53–54
    control of, 53–54
    matching with facial expressions, 54

H

Hagen, Uta, 85
Hilton, Paris, 33

I

improvisation, 67–69
    ABC exercise for, 72
    diction, importance of, 77
    different qualities, physical display of, 72
    emotional changes, displaying, 76
    explore and heighten technique, 74–77
        exercise for, 74

eye contact, importance of, 77
grounding, importance of, 77
loosening up, exercise for, 71
nerves, calming, 76
purposes of, 67–68
questions, avoidance of, 103
skills
    developing, 68–69
    techniques for improving, 78–79
    goals, setting, 78–79
space walk exercise, 72–73
traits for success with, 69
value of, 69
warming up, 69–70
    physical, techniques for, 70
    rhyming exercise for, 78
inflection, impact on vocal variety, 29
inner dialogue
    photo group shots, application to, 135
    photo head shots, application to, 130
inner monologue, application to closing arguments, 115–16

J

jaw issues
    tension in, 24
    stiffness, 20
Jesus Christ, 91
Johnson, Dwayne, 33
Jolie, Angelina, 44, 106
juries, approaches to, 36–38
    adapting to, 89
    addressing the jury, options for, 37
    attention, grabbing, 38
    attitude, choosing, 39–42
        adjustments in, need for, 41–42
        factors involved with, 39
        options for, 39
    body language, analyzing, 36–37
    character, assuming, 39–42
        choices for, 40–42
        exploring through breathing techniques, 42
    concentration, importance of, 42
    connecting with, 89
    creating relationships, 43–44
        choices regarding, 43
    engaging, tips for, 89–90
    juror interest, holding, 38–39
    lively presentations, impact of, 38
    performance expectations of, 98
    relaxation, importance of, 42
    responses, analyzing, 37
    strong openings, benefits of, 37
    voice factors, 42
        breathing exercises, 42
        impact on attitude, 42

K

Kahlo, Frida, 91
King, Larry, 57

L

Letterman, David, 57, 61
lip issues
    lack of mobility, 20
    loosening exercises, 25
listening to yourself, importance of, 4
Longoria, Eva, 60
loudness, gauging, 21–22
    factors in, 21
        audience size, 21
        space size, 21
        topic to be covered, 21

M

McConaughey, Matthew, 44
Meisner, Sanford, 85, 101
Murray, Bill, 91
Myers, Mike, 68

N

natural role, attorneys, 33
   adaptability, need for, 33
   development of, 33
   recognition of, 33
neutral position, 46. *Also see* expression, nonverbal
   benefits of, 46
   defined, 46
   image, impact of, 46
   keys to development of, 47
   posture, 46
      proper, benefits of, 46
      role of, 46
   purpose of, 46

O

Obama, Barack, 54
observation, body language exercise for, 50

P

Pacino, Al, 10, 33
Parker, Charlie, 91
pauses, impact on vocal variety, 28
Perot, H. Ross, 54
photos, posing for group shots, 132–35
   distraction techniques, 135
   get air under your armpits, 134
   inner dialogue, use of, 135
   left shoulder forward, 132
   posture issues, 134
   push your head forward, 133
   shooting from above, 135
photos, posing for head shots, 126
   actable verbs, thinking of, 131–32
   clothing options, 129
   comfort, achieving, 129
   confidence, conveying, 129
   connecting with the camera, 130
   day of shoot preparations, 128–29
   eye factors, 129–30
      inner dialogue, use of, 129
      liveliness, importance of, 129–30
   inner dialogue, use of, 131
   keys to a winning smile, 126–28
   personality, revealing, 128–29
   relaxation exercises for, 130
pitch of speech, impact on vocal variety, 31
Pitt, Brad, 106
pointing, 29–30
   defined, 29
   understanding, 30
   vocal variety, impact on, 29
positive thinking, 8–9
   development of, 8–9
   visualization, relation to, 8
posture, 46
   neutral position, role in, 46
   proper, benefits of, 46
public speaking. *Also see* speech issues
   psychological preparation for, 6–9
      calmness, cultivating, 7
      joke telling, value of, 6–7
      threats, analysis of, 6
      visualization, art of, 8
      positive thinking, relation to, 8–9
   skills, practice of, ongoing need for, 35

R

Reeves, Keanu, 17
relaxation, value of, 24
   exercises for, 24
   jaw, tension in, 24
   lips, loosening of, 25
   tongue, loosening of, 24
relaxed manner, maintaining, 4–5
research of audience, need for, 13
resonance as vocal problem, 21
role playing, 33–34

characters, 90–92
   defining, 34
   selection of, 90
   types of, 91–92
characters,
   juries, application to, 39–42
   value of, 4
   versatility, need for, 33
   witnesses, application to, 103–04
Russert, Tim, 57

S

scrutiny, coping with, 4–5
sense memory and closing arguments, 113
   keys to, 115
   relaxation, importance of, 115
   skills for developing, 114–15
      exercise for, 114
Shatner, William, 44
shell, breaking out of, 15
   animated leader, becoming, 15
   importance of, 15
   small talk, role of, 15
   standing on a chair exercise, 16
Snoop Dogg, 31
speech issues
   overemphatic, hazards of, 20
   rate of, impact on vocal variety, 28
Spielberg, Steven, 38
Spolin, Viola, 120
stage fright, coping with, 120–21
stage presence, 1–13, *Also see* entrances and exits; public speaking; shell, breaking out of; visualization, art of
   actor display of, 10–11
   demonstration of, 2
   development of, 3–4
      listening to yourself, importance of, 4
      sense of calm, use of, 7
      sense of play, use of, 4
   exploration of, need for, 4
   goal of, 5
   impact of, 3
   importance of, 2
   relaxed manner, appearance of, 4–5
   research of audience, need for, 13
   role playing, 4
   scrutiny, coping with, 5
   techniques for learning, 9–10
   tension, release of, 5
   true self, adhering to, 11
      techniques for, 12
   undermining of, 3
      audience, lack of control of, 3
      emergencies, failure to plan for, 3
      lack of confidence, 3
Stanislavski, Constantin, 85
Stein, Ben, 27
Stern, Howard, 57
Stewart, Rod, 48
storytelling, 82–92. *Also see* audience issues
   attorney detachment, hazards of, 83
   cases, treatment of, 83–84
   challenges to, 82
   character, 91–92
      role in, 90
      types of, 91–92
   exercise for, 86
   five-point structure for, 93
   great stories, keys to, 84
   hero, focus on, 90–92
   making up a story, 94
   one-word stories, 92
   preparation for, 93–94
   skills for, importance of, 81
   standard structure, following, 84
   Stanislavski approach to, 85
   truthfulness, role of, 88
Strasberg, Lee, 85

stress, 5
  psychosomatic responses to, 5
  public speaking, cause of, 5

T

tongue, loosening exercises, 24
trial advocacy classes, focus of, 82
true self, adhering to, 11–13
  techniques for, 12

V

visualization, art of, 8–9
  athlete use of, survey on, 9
  detailed scheme, creation of, 9
  positive thinking, relation to, 8
  techniques for-, 8–9
vocal problems, 19–21
  breathiness, 21
  clipped vowels, 20–21
  daily vocal exercises, impact of, 21
  lack of lip mobility, 20
  losing the ends of words, 20
  overemphatic speech, 20
  overexplosive consonants, 20
  poor diction, 20
  stiff jaw, 20
  too much resonance, 21
vocal variety, 27–32
  appearance, impact on 32
  inflection, 29
  pauses, 28–29
  pitch, 31
  pointing, 29–30
    defined, 29
    understanding, 30
  rate of speech, 28
  volume, 30
voice, care of, 31–32
  activities to avoid, 31
  tips for, 31–32
voice, control of, 42
  attitude, application to, 43
  breathing exercises for, 42

volume of speech, impact on vocal variety, 30
vowels, clipping of, 20–21

W

Williams, Robin, 33
Winfrey, Oprah, 57, 60
witness preparation, 97–99
  ambiguous questions, responding to, 101
  behavior outside courtroom, 106
  compound questions, 102
    defined, 102
    responding to, 102
  confusion, coping with, 102
  important things to say on the witness stand, 107
  introductory clauses, importance of, 102
  labeling of witness, controlling, 99
  listening, importance of, 100–01
  overstatements, responding to, 107
  pauses, value of, 108
  questions
    analyzing of, 108
    repeating of, 101
  rehearsals, 104
    topics to cover during, 104
    value of, 104
  role playing during trial, 104
  setting, achieving familiarity with, 98–99
  testimony, delivery of, 100–01
  tips for, 99–09
  trial day, advice for, 105–06
  truthfulness, importance of, 103
  volunteering information, avoidance of, 108–09
witness questioning, techniques for, 62–63
  conferring with attorney, response to, 65

information, eliciting, 64
    exercises for, 65
leading questions, 62
    appropriateness of, 62
    defined, 62
    examples of, 63
open-ended questions
    benefits of, 62
    examples of, 62
tone of voice, importance of, 63

witnesses, relating to, 60–61. *Also see* witness questioning, techniques for
    information, eliciting, 61
    interruptions, avoiding, 61–62
    intimidation, use of, 61
    small talk, use of, 60
    talk, encouragement of, 61
word endings, losing, 20

About the Author

Laura Mathis is a professional public-speaking coach for attorneys and a working actress. She has more than 17 years of experience in theater, film, television, and public speaking as a teacher, actor, writer, and legal performance consultant. She has an honors BFA degree in theatre and drama studies from the University of Toronto and an acting diploma from Sheridan College.

She is the owner of Spotlight Legal and has developed techniques for applying the skills and training utilized by actors to the legal profession. She works extensively with attorneys across the country to help them find their "inner performer" and present their best selve when arguing in the courtroom, negotiating with opposing counsel, or even running for public office.

You can contact Laura at lauramathis@spotlightlegal.com.